Early praise for The Author's Guide to Marketing

"Beth Jusino has created a smart resource for authors who are serious about understanding their marketing responsibilities and who want to take control of building their unique platforms. As a former agent and a longtime editor, she knows what she's talking about – this is a book that will help authors succeed. I love it. In fact, I'm going to be buying copies for my clients!"

— Chip MacGregor, President, MacGregor Literary Agency

"Finally! A smart, functional, and realistic author guide for selling more books. Book insider and marketing expert Beth Jusino nails the challenges authors face in a radically changing publishing environment. This is the only marketing book you need, written by a literary authority who has helped hundreds of authors— including me—get published. Buy Beth's book immediately and benefit from her decades of experience, her clearheaded thinking, and her uncanny ability to help even the most perplexed authors succeed."

— Geoffrey Tumlin, author of *Stop Talking, Start Communicating* and CEO of Mouthpeace Consulting LLC

"In *The Author's Guide to Marketing*, Beth Jusino says '. . . marketing is about understanding your audience, putting yourself in their shoes and understanding what they want.' And she leads by example in accomplishing exactly that in her own book. She recognizes that many writers, like myself, would rather impale themselves on a dull pencil than attempt marketing their novels. Beth's instructive approach is conversational, entertaining, and insightful.

Each chapter ends with questions that, when answered, will lead to a realistic, individualized and do-able marketing plan. Thomas Carruthers said, 'a teacher is one who makes himself progressively unnecessary.' Beth Jusino is one of those teachers."

— Christa Allan, author of *Edge of Grace* and *Test of Faith*

"*The Author's Guide to Marketing* cuts through the clanging cymbals of today's one-size-fits-all marketing advice and points the writer toward a strategy crafted around the author's own strong suits. Filled with in-depth and practical application to make your books and your brand shine, Jusino tackles the mountain that is marketing and makes it a mole-hill."

— J.L. Spohr, author of *Heirs & Spares: A Novel*

"After thirty years in sales and marketing, I was wise enough to hire Beth Jusino to engineer my marketing plan. Her knowledge and marketing savvy was *that* impressive. Now she's put her wit and wisdom into *The Author's Guide to Marketing*, and it should be required reading for every writer. Beth's book is the simplest, easiest, and most fun way to bring your book to market. I've already gone back to it several times for great ideas and new perspectives. You will find it a constant companion, no matter where you are in your writing career."

— Seeley James, author of *Bring It*, a Pia Sabel thriller

"Every writer trying to sell a story should read this book—front to cover—and memorize every concept on every page! Beth Jusino offers a well-researched and practical guide, written in a conversational manner, for authors covering everything they need to know to connect with readers. With relevant information on using (and mis-using) social media platforms, as well as establishing an author brand that means more than a clever quote, Ms. Jusino nails how to build the kind of author platform that showcases books and puts them on bestseller lists! This one will stay on my bookshelves (highlighted, sticky-noted, and underlined in red pen!)"

— Kellie Coates Gilbert, author of *A Woman of Fortune*

"Beth Jusino knows what she's talking about when she says that being a published author today means becoming the CEO of your own start-up business. Authors in today's evolving publishing climate must wear many hats, and one of the most important is that of Chief Marketer. In *The Author's Guide to Marketing*, Beth provides a refreshingly candid resource that will help you tackle the number one, hard-nosed, left-brain oriented business talent you're going to need to be successful as an author: how to market your book in a rapidly evolving marketplace. Beth covers all today's marketing tools: from social media to paid promotion to traditional marketing methods. If you want your new book to do more than simply sit on a shelf (real or digital), *The Author's Guide to Marketing* should be required reading."

— M.D. Grayson, author of the Danny Logan mysteries

"When it comes to marketing in this social media driven world, Beth Jusino breaks it down and helps authors to navigate those waters in our own style and personal bent. Simplify, make a plan, and be yourself is the heart of her message. Read it. And then dive in and take charge of the opportunity to discover and connect with readers galore!"

— Rajdeep Paulus, award-winning author of *Swimming Through Clouds* and *Seeing Through Stones*

"I finished this book kicking myself for the half-dozen simple things I *should have done* before my book release, and eager to get started on a dozen more. And yet Beth Jusino offers much more than an expanded to-do list. She gives authors like me—who are not natural self-promoters—the means and the *permission* to form a plan that plays only to our strengths, without the pressure to follow every new trend or social media site. I am now actually looking forward to marketing my book: on my own terms and, more importantly, at my own pace."

— Christopher Fisher, author of the award-winning *A History of Stone and Steel*

"For many authors, the concept of marketing is like a monster hiding in the closet. We may crack the door for a peek, but fear of the unknown (Will it eat me alive?) sends us running for safety. Beth Jusino's *The Author's Guide to Marketing* offers a hand to hold, a bravery tonic, and a rational approach to demystify that monster. In this witty and concise handbook, you will learn to craft a marketing plan specific to your audience, your project, and your personal strengths. I began applying her suggestions immediately and will be following the customizable template included for the upcoming release of my novel. Whether you're face to face with the marketing monster or still cowering in the corner, *The Author's Guide to Marketing* can help you tame the beast and even learn to enjoy his company."

— Evangeline Denmark, author of *Curio* (releasing 2016)

"If you're looking for a Sherpa for your marketing journey, Beth Jusino is the one. *The Author's Guide to Marketing* is smartly written, witty, and insightful. It's also honest. There's no 'if you build it, they will come' fluff scenarios. This is hard work, and she tells you so. But she also shares real life experiences and gives you the tools to create an effective marketing plan."

— Chris Little, author of *The Darkness of Shadows*

"If you're looking to learn about the reality of marketing your own book, this is the gold standard. I wish I had written it, although if I had, I doubt it'd be this good."

— Paul Jarvis, bestselling author of five books, including *The Good Creative*

the author's guide to marketing

make a plan that attracts more readers and sells
more books (you may even enjoy it)

Beth Jusino

Beth Jusino

SW
SharperWordsPress

The Author's Guide to Marketing
© 2014 Beth Jusino

For more information about this book or the author, visit http://bethjusino.com

ISBN 978-0-9903351-0-8
eISBN 978-0-9903351-1-5

First edition 2014
Printed in the United States of America

Sharper Words Press
A division of Sharper Words, LLC
PO Box 20681
Seattle, WA 98102

Email books@sharperwords.com

Disclaimer: All the examples and stories in this book are true, but names and identifying details have been changed to protect both the innocent and the guilty, and to prevent the need for endless rounds of legal permission paperwork. Most are compiled from multiple author experiences, so if you think you see yourself on one of these pages, rest assured that at least two other writers are thinking the same thing about the same example.

Cover design by Kelly Leslie
Interior design by Eric Jusino

*For every writer who invited me to be part of your
journey to publication*

(and for a few who didn't, but should have)

Contents

1

---

who, me?

"To write what is worth publishing, to find honest people to publish it, and get sensible people to read it, are the three great difficulties in being an author." — Charles Caleb Colton

So here you are. You have taken—or are about to take, or you're thinking about taking—the step from solitary writer working in obscurity to published author[1] with a book that strangers will read. Perhaps you've got an agent (or you're looking for one), a publisher (see previous note), or you've made the decision to self publish. Your book may already be out, or you may still be a year or more from holding it in your hands.

---

[1] Okay, let's get this out of the way right now: if your book is available for sale in some retail channel where strangers can buy it, you're published. Whether you're getting the support of a big New York house, a small university press, a startup that doesn't pay advances, a shady vanity press, or you're doing it all yourself, you're published. Whether you had great editing or no editing, whether your book sells two million copies or two copies, you're published. There are lots of other issues that come into play based on the choices you made along the way, but for the sake of these conversations, we're all published authors who want to attract more readers. So let's all stop sniping at one another's choices and move on.

You have discovered that publishing is a long and sometimes winding path. And there's a lot more to it than you probably expected.

You have joined the ranks of writers and artists and inventors who have gone before you, with an exciting new product in hand and a similarly bewildered expression on their faces.

"I've made this thing. Now what?"

And now you're here, reading a book about marketing, wondering how this fits into your dream to write a great novel (or memoir, or self-help book, or whatever has captured your passion).

To be a writer, all you need to do is write. But being a published author means becoming the CEO of a startup business—the Business of Author You. Your product is your book. There are contracts to sign, partners and contractors to manage, decisions to make about artwork and copyright and the pesky serial comma. And then there's marketing.

You're still getting used to calling yourself an author. Now you're supposed to be a marketer too?

Yep. Congratulations!

No, seriously.

If you approach it the right way, this marketing thing can be an opportunity, not a chore. In fact, if you give me a chance, I'll show you how you might even enjoy your role as Chief Marketer of You.

What this book is—and what it isn't

The Author's Guide to Marketing will help you make a plan that fits *your* style, *your* audience, and *your* available time, talents, and resources.

What's important to understand up front is that every successful author strategy looks different. Sorry, but there is no "secret formula to success" or "30-Day Roadmap That Will Guarantee Your Spot on the Bestseller List." Those headlines belong on the tabloid rack with "The Miracle Diet That Will Make You into a Supermodel in 10 Days." Building an audience that will support your new career as an author isn't going to be as easy as scheduling a book giveaway on the right date or sending a press release to the right channel. What worked for that last best-selling young adult/business expert/e-book/Amish vampire author isn't going to work the same way for you.

Every book, and every author, is different. Therefore, every marketing plan should be different. What works for me in promoting and selling this book about marketing won't necessarily work for a historical fiction writer, and with the speed of today's technology, new opportunities will emerge between the time I'm writing this in 2014 and the time you read it. Timing is important. Trends and technology are fickle. Personalities affect our effectiveness as marketers. And not every audience is eagerly waiting in every marketing channel.

My job is to help you understand what will work for *you* and *your* audience, so that you attract more readers, sell more books, and are not miserable while you do it.

Some of knowing what will work is also understanding what won't. So let me start by giving you permission to say no.

If Twitter makes you miserable, don't do it.

If walking into a bookstore and introducing yourself to the manager makes your head spin, look for other ways to seek retail support.

If being interviewed leaves you speechless, then don't hire a publicist to get you interviews.

If you want to launch your author career, you need to do *something* (actually, a series of somethings), but you don't need to try everything.

Marketing works when it's authentic, and in this day of fragmented audiences and multiple communication channels, every author can find a strategy that fits his or her unique talents and audience. I've intentionally included ideas and resources to help you build an effective marketing strategy both online and offline. While I believe that every published author today needs to be comfortable browsing, communicating, and shopping online (see the epilogue for a longer exploration of this), I don't think that means all good book marketing happens online. Pay attention to what ideas and strategies resonate with you. Your success will come from the areas where you and your audience are most comfortable.

How do I know all of this? Because I've been working with authors to launch their careers and promote their books for almost twenty years, since back in the dark ages before Amazon. I've been a literary agent, an editor, and a ghostwriter. At each step, I saw how important it was for authors to know how to reach their readers, and to be willing to actively share their books. Then a few years ago I partnered with The Editorial Department, a company with a thirty-year reputation of quality and integrity working with writers,[2] to develop an author and book marketing program that would help any writer who wanted to see his or her book in print or pixels.

I've helped hundreds of authors—fiction and nonfiction, self published, traditionally published, small-press published, co-published, and e-published—work out how to build platforms, reach readers, and sell books. Some of them have been spectacularly successful. Others have generated nothing but disappointment.

I want you to have the tools to be part of the former group.

This book is divided into two parts: the first helps you establish a long-term view of your audience, your platform, and the reputation you want to establish. The second part looks at how to use that knowledge to help launch and support a book.

There are questions at the end of each chapter, and in chapter 10 I've included a template for you to create your own marketing plan.

I don't want to just tell you what to do—I want to tell you why you're making the choices you're making, and then let you decide for yourself how to implement the plan. The challenge may seem overwhelming at times. When it seems like there's too much to think about, remember that book marketing, like book writing, is a marathon, not a sprint. It takes time to develop momentum, and you don't need to do everything at one time.

Hide-and-seek on the bookstore shelves

So why does all of this matter?

It used to be that the most difficult part of being published was writing something that would catch the attention of an agent and/or publisher. You'd send dozens, sometimes hundreds, of queries and then

---

[2]Shout out to The Editorial Department (http://editorialdepartment.com), a source of quality editing and publishing support, as well as marketing services.

weather seasons of rejection while you polished the work and improved your craft. If you were chosen, you were set. Your agent would arrange a contract with a publisher, which in turn would produce the book, and then share it with the retailer (typically a bookstore), which in turn would present the book, with their implicit recommendation, to the reader. Your competition, defined as the other books on the store shelf, was limited. Sales were influenced by talent or luck. If the book sold, the author was invited to write again. If not, the book was quickly shuffled to "out of print," and we never heard from those authors again.

Sure, the author may be called on to emerge from his writing garret to go on a book tour (paid for by the publisher) or chat with a newspaper reporter covering the book beat (remember those?). Active authors would schedule speaking engagements (for which they were well paid) to increase their visibility. But the publisher handled the day-to-day business of getting blurbs and book reviews and attracted journalists who were hungry for stories. Readers didn't expect to hear from writers in between books; there was a mystique to preserve. The writers were left to write, living on advances that would never recoup, and treating publishers like they were patrons of the arts, not investors.[3]

At least that's how we all remember the good old days. We conveniently forget the writers who were abandoned in the old model, their books pushed out of print when a publishing staff turned over or an inexperienced publicist dropped the ball and cost them those critical first weeks of sales. Or those writers who never even found the right agent or publisher for their good, but offbeat, book. When authors were dependent on a whole chain of outsiders to ensure their success or failure, there was a lot that they couldn't control.

Today, it's still hard—and maybe harder—for a writer to get that first publishing contract. But even when they do, publishers can't guarantee the same kind of brick-and-mortar placement that they once did. Retailers are either too big (Walmart) or too scarce (the number of independent bookstores has shrunk by 12% in the past 10 years),[4] and media is too

---

[3]This is another rant of mine, which probably doesn't belong in the introduction. I'll talk more about my take on traditional publishing, publisher marketing efforts, and the finances of book publishing, in the epilogue.

[4]Open Education Database, "12 Stats on the State of Bookstores in America Today," http://oedb.org/ilibrarian/12-stats-on-the-state-of-bookstores-in-america-today/.

scattered for there to be a clear way for a new book to gain traditional sales traction.

The real challenge of modern publishing is what we call "discoverability." It's too easy to get lost in those endless shelves of obscurity. When readers are faced with an almost limitless collection of titles, they can't—and won't—sift through all the options to spontaneously discover an unknown voice. Someone needs to help them find the book.

And that someone is the person who cares most about the book's success: the author.

Whether you're a novelist self publishing three fantasy titles a year from your home in Tennessee or a business consultant pitching your proposal to top educational publishers in New York, today you have more influence over how and when your readers find you, and whether they commit to you, than ever before.

Yes, you have to market, even if you're a novelist. Even if you have a publisher. Even if you don't want to.

There's still a lot of luck and good timing tied to breakout success, but your writing career is more firmly in your control than ever before. And so is your marketing.

Let's make that a glass-half-full opportunity.

Why does this matter?

"The only thing that is constant is change," said the Greek philosopher Heraclitus, in a phrase that's been pulled out approximately nine million times in the past 2,500 years, because things keep changing. Right now, the foundations of publishing are in a constant state of change.

You may have heard that this is the best time in history to be a writer. And it's true. Authors have more opportunities to reach readers than ever before, and if they want more control of the process, they can have it. Distribution changes have made almost every book in print available to every reader, wherever they are and whenever they want it. Online bookstore shelves are limitless and global. Print-on-demand technology makes it possible to keep a book in print forever. Finite bookstore shelf space or the demands of scale no longer limit publishing.

On the other hand, this is possibly also the hardest time in history to be a successful author, at least if you define success by profit. Reading rates remain flat in the United States, with only three-quarters of all adults reporting that they've read a book in the previous twelve months.[5] But developing technologies and expanding catalogs mean that readers are spread out over more titles than ever. It's easy for a book to get lost in a seemingly limitless catalog of titles, which is growing mind-blowingly fast. In 2012 alone, more than half a million new books were published in the United States—double what released in 2002.[6] And those are just the new books. Amazon.com, the largest single book retailer in the United States, lists more than 12 million titles.

And that doesn't even begin to explore the distractions that readers face from TV, movies, games, and the Internet. We live in a fragmenting society where there's an entertainment niche option for every person, but little that's shared experience.

Publishing got easy, but finding readers got hard.

You can close your car trunk

If this new world of publishing sounds frightening—or horrible—to you, you're not alone. Once a week I have a conversation with an author who says, "But I hate self-promotion! I don't want to go ask people to buy my book!" The good news is that marketing (mostly) isn't about direct sales. No one will ask you to stand on a street corner trying to unload a car trunk full of books like they're Girl Scout cookies, or auto-post awkward "buy my book" messages every hour on Twitter. (Please, don't auto-post awkward "here's a #link to buy my #book!!!" messages every hour on Twitter. That NEVER works.)

Marketing guru Peter Drucker said, "The aim of marketing is to make selling superfluous."

---

[5] Katharyn Zickuhr and Lee Rainie, "A Snapshot of Reading in America in 2013," Pew Research Internet Project, http://www.pewinternet.org/2014/01/16/a-snapshot-of-reading-in-america-in-2013/.

[6] R.R. Bowker, "ISBN Output Report for 2002-2012," http://www.bowker.com/assets/downloads/products/isbn_output_2002_2012.pdf.

Marketing is nothing more or less than building positive public awareness about your name and your books.

That sounds innocent enough.

But when we look at how books are sold, the process rarely feels innocent. Why?

Because too many authors are doing it wrong.

They're ignoring their audience.

They're chasing the fads.

They're trying to be people they're not.

You've seen them. They're the writers who pop up on every social media channel, following and being followed by other writers, and posting an almost incomprehensible series of links and exclamation points. They shove postcard-size ads for their books into your hand the first time they meet you, before they've even asked your name. They blog sporadically only about their own books. They release new books one after the other, but the reviews complain about poor writing, and their covers seem to have been thrown together by an eight-year-old with a penchant for dated photos and flowery fonts.[7]

If you've dipped a toe into the writing and publishing world, you know who I'm talking about.

On the other side, there are authors who are doing it wrong in different ways.

They're ignoring their readers.

They're chasing the illusion of being spontaneously discovered.

They're not becoming the successful authors they can be.

You probably *haven't* seen these writers, or their books. They're waiting quietly at home for the phone to ring, watching their Amazon sales rank plummet into the millions, while their royalty statements stubbornly refuse to rise above single digits. They like to complain about their lack of sales, but they haven't looked at their own website in months, let alone updated it. Their attempt at marketing was to send one mass email to everyone they've ever met, telling them to "go to Amazon and type my book title into the search engine."

---

[7]No, I'm not picking on self-published authors here. I've also seen some hideous traditionally published covers.

Different approaches, different mistakes. But in the end, the same outcome: disappointment.

It doesn't have to be like that.

Here's what author marketing can be like:

You can know your audience and give them something they want.

You can use your strengths and stretch yourself in the places you want to grow.

You can be an author who's connected to an active, supportive community of readers.

That doesn't sound so bad.

Your marketing work as an author should be natural to who you are and what your audience wants. It should feel genuine and trustworthy.

It should be...easy?

Okay, not easy as in "Hey, I don't need to put any effort into this, and stuff just happens!"

Easy as in "Hey, this doesn't suck. Sure, I have to put time into it, but it's not unpleasant time. And sometimes I'm actually having fun!"

Establishing the right marketing plan should be like putting on the right hiking shoes before you climb a mountain: you'll still have to do the work to drag yourself to the top, and depending on how out of shape you are (face it, we writers are not known for our aerobic endurance), you're going to sweat. But the right shoes protect you. They prevent blisters and turned ankles. With good support, you can walk farther, faster. They make the long climb...*easier.*

And that's what *The Author's Guide to Marketing* is about.

It's natural to be afraid of this. But if you are smart and talented enough to write a book, you are absolutely capable of working through the questions and checklists on the following pages and of developing and capitalizing on your own author marketing campaign. Take it one step at a time.

And perhaps even have some fun with it.

Let's get started.

part one

diving right in

In which I horribly overuse a pool metaphor to help you understand how to evaluate, define, and build an author platform for long-term marketing.

part one

diving right in

2

how big is your pool?

"Make the customer the hero of your story." — Ann Handley

"I would be a liar, a hypocrite, or a fool—and I'm not any of those—to say that I don't write for the reader. I do. But for the reader who hears, who really will work at it, going behind what I seem to say. So I write for myself and that reader who will pay the dues." — Maya Angelou

Susan used to write romance novels. She published half a dozen books with a small press that sold their stories via a subscription model, and she honed her writing craft. But then the publisher closed its doors, and Susan was left without a contract. (This scenario is all too familiar to any writer publishing in the 2000s.)

Susan floundered for a bit, but then happened to have lunch with a friend who told her a funny story about a neighbor's goat. The tale inspired Susan, who had been an elementary school librarian years ago. So she cracked open her laptop and started a chapter book starring a goat. Susan's agent helped her land a contract with a new house for a four-book series featuring her goat. And just like that, Susan was a children's book writer.

In the past, Susan's approach to author marketing had been to publish regularly, to be an active member of Romance Writers of America, and to keep up a website and regular email newsletter to her fans. But her mailing list was made up of women who wanted spicy tidbits and romantic fantasies. They weren't going to care about a goat. And her new audience definitely shouldn't see some of her racy early work.

Even though Susan was an established author, changing her audience meant that her entire marketing approach needed to change, too. That's because the audience is the heart of every marketing project, and the first question you must ask, as early in the publishing process as possible, is this:

Who will want to read my book?

This is the single most important question that you will answer in developing your author marketing plan. (Not to put any pressure on your answer or anything.)

Your readers are the center of your publishing career. They should be the first and central focus of every publishing-related thought you have. They are the reason you're doing all of this. If they don't exist, then you may as well leave that manuscript on your hard drive.

Everything you do to release and promote your book, and hopefully throughout your publishing career, will depend on understanding your primary readers.

There's no space in modern publishing for narcissist authors. If you have an idea that doesn't support your readers, if it doesn't appeal to them, if it doesn't build your connection to them, then it doesn't matter.

Because if you don't know who you're writing for, no amount of marketing effort will reach them.

I ask every author I work with to "tell me about your primary reader, the person who will be the most attracted to your book." All too often the answer I get is some variation of "Everyone likes my book. It will appeal to women and men, from their teens all the way to senior citizens."

Sorry, wrong answer.

Even the Bible, arguably the most widely read book in human history, has a more targeted primary readership than that.[1]

If an author hasn't thought deeply about his readers and doesn't have a basic understanding of who he is and what he's looking for, that's a sign that the author isn't digging deep enough. He's the one who will likely waste time and money shouting into a void, trying to promote his books in ways that no one will hear. Don't be him.

Because let's face it, you can't market to "everyone." You probably don't have the budget to rent billboards all over the country, or the time to knock on every single door, or mail an ad with your book cover to every single person. (Even if you did, that would be kind of creepy.) And while standing on top of a roof and yelling, "Hey, I wrote a book!" might look like you're doing something, in reality it doesn't reach anyone.

Think that's a ridiculous example? Authors do the equivalent every day. Does it really make sense to pay for a website, but then hope that the right people just happen to find it? Or to pay a publicist thousands of dollars to send generic press releases to media outlets that never cover your type of book? Or to travel the country to visit local bookstores if your audience doesn't shop in brick-and-mortar outlets? And when you consider that only 18% of Americans use Twitter (albeit a disproportionately influential 18%), it's worth thinking about whether your readers fit the demographic before you spend too much time learning to be effective there.[2]

Defining your core audience doesn't limit your book marketing—it informs it. It helps you prioritize where to spend your time and resources and influences everything from your cover design to where your book is shelved in bookstores.

---

[1] The Bible, including the Old and New Testaments, is primarily targeted toward Christian readers, and secondarily toward those who are interested in learning about Christianity. While the marketers of the Bible may hope that it will appeal to "everyone," selling it to devout atheists, Muslims, or Buddhists takes more effort.

[2] Does it seem like I'm picking on Twitter? I don't mean to. I personally love Twitter (@bethjusino) and have successfully used it to market. But it's also the channel that seems to intimidate the most authors, who think they "have" to use it, and so it's the channel I often see misused.

Think about the first 100 strangers who will buy your book. Every project is different, but audience demographics can often be defined by:

- Preferred book genres (e.g., readers who enjoy legal thrillers)

- Gender

- Age

- Social or religious views

- Geography (i.e., do they mostly live in a certain region?)

- Other non-reading hobbies (e.g., fans of a certain TV show, horse-back riders, gardeners)

- Education

- Family status (e.g., single women, parents of young children, divorced men)

- Felt need (i.e., if they are seeking an answer to a question, what's the question?)

(*Note*: These are examples of ways to look at an audience, but not every category will apply to every author's audience. If you write science fiction, for example, your audience won't have a strong regional appeal, but non-reading hobbies definitely must be considered. On the other hand, if you are writing a memoir about growing up in the Alaskan wilderness, you'll find a concentration of interested book buyers in Alaskan bookstores.)

If you're having trouble focusing on the reader by demographic, try this: Picture your book on a bookstore shelf. What section is it in? Who's naturally browsing there? Those are the people who are looking for the kind of book you write. That's your audience, in the broadest sense.[3]

So if you're writing fiction, the first level of your target audience is always "people who read fiction." This is true regardless of what your

---

[3] Understanding your genre isn't the same as identifying specific comparative titles or authors, which you may have struggled with if you tried to write a book proposal. Right now, focus on the broader question of category: what shelf will your book be on in the bookstore? When you browse on Amazon or other online bookstores, where in the category menu would you find your book?

novel is about. It's highly unusual for a person who doesn't usually read fiction to pick up a novel because they're interested in the topic, but novel readers will follow the type of book they love (thriller, romance, women's fiction) to all sorts of imaginative new settings. If you're writing an erotic thriller about a female pianist in the sixteenth century, your primary audience will be erotica readers, not people who are interested in Mozart, even if the composer makes a cameo appearance. When you're considering your marketing options, a press release to the Mozart Fan Club of Vienna shouldn't be at the top of your list.

Not knowing your genre can be disastrous for your project. I know an author—let's call him Jim—who wrote a coming-of-age story with a thirteen-year-old boy, set in the early 1980s. Jim attracted an agent who said he was excited about the book, but then proceeded to try to sell it to publishers and editors of young adult fiction. The reasoning? Jim's protagonist was a teenager; therefore, the book must be written for teenagers. The problem? The character's journey wasn't something that was written to appeal to contemporary teenagers, and the publishers knew that teen readers wouldn't be interested in someone who was a teen before they were born. While they complimented the writing, they all turned it down.

Jim's audience wasn't young adults; it was the thirty-and forty-something Generation X readers who would see their own coming-of-age stories in the young protagonist. When Jim finally split with his agent and self published his book as adult fiction, the sales took off.[4]

There are other red flags to avoid when considering your audience:

- *"My readers will be the people who need to understand that the way they're living is wrong. I'll offer them a better way to see themselves/their husbands/their pets/their jobs."* Writers often fall into the trap of thinking about who they *want* to reach, instead of who they *will* reach. Readers only become book buyers if they're natu-

---

[4]This anecdote is also a good reminder that you can't abdicate your own responsibility to understand your audience if you have an agent, publisher, or other partner. Professionals are smart and good at what they do (well, most of them), but they have their own biases, and they miss things, too. If you think your agent or publisher is pushing your book to the wrong audience, speak up. If you don't agree on that first part, it can all go downhill quickly.

rally interested in the content, so if your stated purpose is to alter someone's perspective, then your readers must be people who are open to some kind of change, not those who are comfortable where they are. I see this most often with self-help and inspirational books that aren't written to meet a specific felt need, but I've seen authors' ulterior motives shadow the marketing of everything from cookbooks to romance fiction. That's not to say that you can't have a motive in writing—humor novelist Carl Hiassen has probably done more to raise awareness of the environmental troubles of Florida than any nonfiction writer ever could—but you'll need to understand that your goals are not necessarily your reader's goals. When you're thinking about marketing, focus on what your reader wants—an exciting story, a practical way to live better, an artfully crafted experience, an escape—and deliver that before anything else.

- *"Even though this type of person doesn't usually read books like this, they'll still like..."* Stop. If your target reader isn't naturally inclined to your genre, they won't be your first readers. After a book is released and develops a following, the demographics may shift and grow via word of mouth. The Harry Potter series, for example, was originally released for middle-school children, a decision that affected everything from the story length and writing style to the cover design. As the reputation of the stories spread and people started to talk about the intricate plotting and imaginative characters, the audience expanded to adults who never would have expected to be reading children's fantasy. But that kind of growth takes time and only happens if the project blows away the initial audience. Don't focus your early marketing on the hard sells.

- *"Everyone who's read my manuscript loves it. Even my father, who never reads romance novels, said he couldn't put it down."* Yes, writers do say this to me, and no, it doesn't work that way. You should *never* define your target reader based on the responses of people you know. Period. Ever. Your relationship with them influences their feedback, no matter how hard they try to be objective. When you picture your target audience, they should always be people you don't know. After all, the purpose of publishing is to get your book past your immediate circle and to people you've never met.

How big is the pool?

The potential size of your initial audience will depend on your book. Statistically, there are more people who read romance than who read modern literary fiction. There are fewer people looking for information about a specific esophageal disease than there are people who want to know how to lose weight. Your book sales will likely reflect that.

This doesn't mean that you should automatically try to write or market to the largest demographics or the most popular topics. Where there are more readers, there's also more competition. As I was writing this, Amazon.com listed more than 60,000 titles in the "Mystery" fiction section, but only 600 in "Mythology/Folklore." So if your book is a creative re-telling of an ancient Indian legend about a murder, you'll probably find your more dedicated, interested audience in the smaller pool, where the competition for top spots isn't so fierce.

The bigger the pool, the harder it is for an emerging author to make a big splash.

Not only that, but if marketing is going to be a project you enjoy, it's important to write for a group that you like. If you write a young adult novel because you see them selling well, but don't like teenagers and never read young adult fiction, you're setting yourself up for a bumpy ride. The whole purpose of building an author platform (discussed in chapter 4) is to regularly and authentically connect with readers, to get their attention and earn their loyalty. When you define your audience, get ready to spend a lot of time in their world.

These considerations all worked out well for Susan, whose stories about goats led her to a new audience of elementary-school-aged children—and by default, the parents, teachers, and librarians who are purchasers and decision makers for that group. Yes, she needed to start over with her marketing efforts as she moved to a whole new pool, but given her previous experience as a teacher and her general love for children, the idea of interacting with young readers excited her, and she could throw herself into a new marketing strategy.

Does your audience excite you?

Where does your audience gather?

Once you've identified who your early readers and followers will be and what they care about, push yourself deeper to think about where to find them. Your future readers—the ones who haven't yet heard of your book, but will love it when they do—are already congregating around books, websites, and events that interest them.

The busy mom who loves cookbooks travels in different circles from the teenager who immerses himself in dystopian fantasy novels. They not only read different books, but they also visit different websites, have different friends, and communicate in different ways.

If you can pinpoint some of those places, your platform-building and book marketing efforts can go to them, instead of waiting for them to come to you.

What do older, conservative readers who like to read clean romances do when they're not reading? You'll find many of them in churches or community gatherings. Those middle-aged, recently single women on the verge of re-entering the dating pool after a divorce? Social media and dating websites, maybe self-help events. Those disillusioned twenty-somethings who appreciate dark humor? They've found the coolest new Internet TV shows, the independent web comics, and the best of whatever's new in emerging multimedia.

When you think about where readers gather, consider "live" options, as well as online networks. What are they doing when they're sitting in front of their computers, and what do they do when their computers are off?

If you are writing a travel memoir about a year you spent volunteering for an orphanage in Africa, your readers may be socially conscious and globally aware young adults who are looking for ideas about how they can make a difference in the world. They come together online in progressive discussion groups and social networking areas where they can share articles and live vicariously through others' stories. They volunteer for local outreach programs and they attend events that support programs they care about. As travelers or wannabe travelers, their technology is mobile. They have tablet computers and listen to podcasts. They read blogs. They love (love, love!) photos.

If you are writing romance, your readers are primarily women, both married and single, older than thirty-five. If they gather online, it's primarily on basic social media sites like Facebook, image-sharing sites like Pinterest, and book-focused sites like Amazon and Goodreads. Serious romance readers connect on blogs specifically dedicated to romance reviews. (Romance readers are voracious readers, and they love to talk about the books they read.) They form tight communities and relationships, follow favorite authors loyally, and love informal chat. Because they're voracious readers, they're also likely e-reader fans and buy most of their books online. Offline, there aren't many book-related ways to find romance readers, but look for regional festivals and writer's conferences, or "Girls' Night Out" events and weekend retreats.

Once you have a basic profile of your readers, take the time to explore and engage in their worlds—not to market or to actively promote or sell anything, but to research and observe. Browse websites, subscribe to blogs and read the comments as well as the posts, and think about what questions are being asked. Attend lectures about retirement savings if you're a financial writer, or go to Comic-Con if you're working on a graphic novel. If you're writing your own family history, join a genealogy group. If you want your novel to appeal to book clubs, then join a book club.

This is your pool. Get comfortable in it.

Your turn

Who is your audience?

- What are their basic demographics? Define this by age, gender, religion, geography, socioeconomic status, politics, or anything else that is appropriate for your project.

- What are the books that are currently on their desks or bedside tables? What do they love to read? Get specific and name three or four titles or authors. (Keep these titles contemporary, preferably published in the past three years; if your target reader is immersed in the complete works of Hemingway, you may have a hard time convincing her to try something new.)

- What do they do when they are not reading? Are they parents caught up in the day-to-day schedules and carpools? Are they travelers (or armchair travelers) who fill their free time learning about distant places? Are they committed to their faith communities?

- When they get in the car and turn on the radio, what are they listening to?

- Where do they get their news?

- How often do they go online every day, and what do they do when they're there?

3

---

are you ready to swim with the sharks?

"A person who publishes a book willfully appears before the populace with his pants down... If it's a good book, nothing can harm her. If it's a bad book, nothing can help her." — *Edna St. Vincent Milay*

"The self-edited author is as foolish as the self-medicated patient." — *Guy Kawasaki*

Are you enjoying yourself yet? Hopefully you're starting to see how marketing, when we look at it as *the building of positive public awareness about you and your books,* can be accessible, not intimidating. Maybe you're even a little excited about spending more time interacting with your readers and deepening your involvement in the communities you've invested so much writing time for.

But you are, after all, the Chief Marketer of You, and a business doesn't just exist to build a community. There's a purpose for you to do all of this, and that's to attract more people and sell more copies of your flagship product: your book.

So before we start looking at specific marketing tools, let's talk about your book.

Earlier this week I had a tough call with a client, a man who's passionate about sharing a message. He wanted me to help him develop a query letter that would attract a publisher. After reading his manuscript, I had to tell him the bad news: his subject was interesting and marketable, but his writing was "too undeveloped for professional publication." Yes, those are the stilted, business-ese words I used. I'm not proud of it. But it was the nicest way I could think of to say, "This is so disorganized, stilted, and grammatically challenged that it's practically unreadable."

The writer had the passion for his audience, but he hadn't yet developed the skills to write a book for them. I recommended that he step back, join a critique group or work with a book coach, and spend at least a year, maybe two, developing his writing craft, and then return to the book.

It was a tough message for him to hear, and not a fun one for me to deliver. "Won't the publisher pay for an editor after they sign the book?" he pleaded.

Sorry, but no. Not for a project that needed that much work. Not unless he'd been featured on the cover of last week's *People* magazine. (And even then, they'd make him pay for his own ghostwriter.) Publishers are not in the business of finding ugly ducklings and then financially supporting their makeovers into swans. Especially now, with tighter budgets, lower margins, and a steady stream of eager new writers with polished projects ready to go, publishers can only afford to use their editorial teams to fine tune and polish a manuscript, not to overhaul it.

Of course, if you are your own publisher, you don't even have the luxury of falling back on the "gatekeeper" experience of classic publishing. It's entirely up to you to decide when your product is ready to be launched to the public. There's nothing between you and the final arbiter of your success: the readers.

Are you really ready for them?

No, seriously. You need to believe this.

Did you write a good book?

Is it captivating in concept and well-crafted in prose?

Has it fully matured?

Every good marketing plan is based on the assumption that the business has something worthwhile to market, so we need to stop at this point and take a serious look at the product that The Business of You is selling.

If you write a book that readers love, they will share their experiences and recommend it to others. But if readers are frustrated by the product's quality—no matter how great the concept, cover design, ad campaign, or list of endorsers is—they'll quickly let it fall into an abyss of silence. No reviews. No media. No recommendations. Without positive feedback, unpolished books slide into obscurity, their market devoured and their readers distracted by more popular titles. And no amount of money or time will drag those obscure titles back out.

Well, that sounds dire. How can we avoid that?

First, by taking time to learn the craft of writing, and doing it right. And second, by understanding that you are a lousy judge of your own writing.

10,000 hours

In his controversial book *Outliers: The Story of Success*, Malcolm Gladwell says that it takes 10,000 hours to learn a skill, and writing is definitely a skill. We're not born knowing how to build tension page after page, or how to organize a series of thoughts into a persuasive work.

Have you put in your 10,000 hours?

When technology made publishing quick and easy, people started acting as if the pace of writing had changed as well. There's a constant state of rush among some writers now, a looming pressure to finish the book and publish it as soon as possible, either so the author can start earning money, or so no one else publishes the idea first,[1] or just to see the book finished. I've met more than a few writers who tell me that they decided to publish because they were tired of writing and revising. They were so sick of the book they wanted it to go away.

That's a lousy reason to put a product into consumer hands.

Releasing half a million books a year has created what author Lee Goldberg, himself an enthusiastic self-published author, calls "a tsunami of swill" filling online bookstore shelves: nonfiction titles that are so disorganized I can't tell by the end what the author wanted me to know, novels that have no more sense of plot and character than my weekly grocery list, memoirs of unique experiences lost in sloppy writing.

I love books, and my heart hurts to read a published manuscript and see the unreached potential. But even worse, as a marketing professional, I grieve for the poor author who's now stuck trying to promote a book that was born prematurely.

Your marketing efforts started, whether you knew it or not, as soon as the first draft of your manuscript was done. The time and effort you put into your revisions, the level of care and attention you gave to your craft, is the biggest tool in your marketing belt. Because if you can't win over those early readers, no amount of time or money will help the book.[2]

Would you be willing to put your book up against the best-selling work in its genre?

Because that's what happens when you publish. A reader will choose between your legal thriller and John Grisham's. Between your book on

---

[1] This concern about publishing "first" is something that comes up often with aspiring authors but is an unnecessary concern. Whatever your idea is, whether it's history or health, science fiction or poetry, someone has published something like it before, and someone will probably publish something like it after you do. That's okay. No one will be writing about your topic in exactly the same way you are: no one has your perspective. And readers who are interested in a topic or genre don't typically limit themselves to only one book on a subject. For example, there seem to be several dozen books about author marketing currently listed on Amazon, but I'm not worried about adding another one. There's obviously reader demand for the information, and no other author has the same perspective and experiences that I do.

[2] Yes, I know there are plenty of wildly successful books out there that seem mediocre. Life's sometimes unfair like that. But it's also worth noting that no matter how much we complain about the ways certain authors write about vampires or kinky sex or medieval conspiracies, those books usually have a strong sense of style and emotional appeal that perfectly align with what their target audiences want.

what makes a healthy marriage and one written by a psychologist with her own daytime talk show.

(When I say this, I am making an assumption that you've done your market research, and you've not only stopped to understand your genre, as we discussed in the previous chapter, but also sampled the most popular books that your reader is reading. You should be actively reading the best-selling books in your genre and reviewing book reviews of both popular and debut authors in your genre to get a better sense of how readers react to different styles and stories. We cannot write what we don't know.)

Your readers are savvy, and they're powerful. Word of mouth has never been so important, so public, or so easy to track.

In the days before the Internet, if readers were dissatisfied with a book, they could write the publisher a letter. Now they blog about it and call you out on Twitter.

If readers were frustrated by a book's slow start, when "nothing had happened" fifty pages in, or the book had serious proofreading errors, readers used to simply put the book down. Maybe they'd tell a handful of friends. If they were really upset, they might take it back to the bookstore and demand a refund. Their experience might affect your sales in a single area. Now readers can go to Amazon and share their displeasure with the world. Every person who looks at your book page will see that "iluvbunnies21" couldn't get through chapter 3, and they'll wonder if the book in worth their time.

Are you ready to swim with the sharks?

I have friends who love to scuba dive. They go almost every weekend to swim in the frigid Puget Sound, and they vacation on boats in exotic spots where they can practically roll out of bed and into coral reefs. Their photos are amazing. But they didn't naturally know how to dive. They couldn't buy some equipment, put on a wetsuit, and start swimming with the octopi. It took months for instructors to teach them how to think about breathing in a whole new way. They joined groups of divers with enough experience to show them the best underwater nooks and crannies, and the dangerous caves and cliffs to avoid.

My friends now can, literally, swim with the sharks. But that didn't happen overnight.

Are you ready to swim with your own literary sharks?

I thought I was. This book compiles lessons I've learned over years of working with authors on their marketing programs and platforms. Surely I know everything there is to know, right? Hardly. I sent the first draft to ten writers I know and trust—some published, some still working on getting published—and asked for feedback. They ripped it apart with pages of notes, questions I missed, and things I said that made me sound dumb. And then my copyeditor caught dozens of additional mistakes that, if they'd slipped through, would have made you cringe and wonder whether this marketing expert author had any idea what she was doing.

Writing is a solitary experience, but it takes more than one person to make a great book.

By the time you've put in those 10,000 hours to hone your craft and tell your story, you have stopped being an objective reader of your own work. You need other people to help you see what's working and what still needs work in your manuscript.

Whatever you do, don't trust the evaluation of your manuscript to a family member or friend. The people who eat Thanksgiving dinner with you cannot offer unbiased feedback.

In years past, those "other people" were often the agents and publishers who nurtured and developed a writer's talent for years before they saw a penny for their efforts. For better or for worse (better for all those writers who weren't chosen, maybe worse for those who were), authors and readers can no longer count on publishing professionals to make that kind of costly investment. Agents and publishers today are inundated with submissions at a rate that would have been incomprehensible fifty years ago.[3] As a result, they can be selective, and choose the projects

---

[3]It's not that agents (or publishers) are trying not to open the gates; it's that for most of them there physically isn't room to take on more. When I was an agent, I was part of a four-person agency that was well known in our particular niche, and perhaps not-so-well known beyond that. We had specific rules for submissions, and yet we still received more than 3,000 queries a year. A professional agent can reasonably manage a few dozen active clients at a time, and most agents spend their time working with career authors they've already signed. You do the math.

that are already polished and publishable, rather than ones that show "potential."

So how do you know if your project is ready? By learning from those who have gone before you.

I can't emphasize enough how important it is to read other authors and books in your chosen genre. And don't just read them—study them. Pick up the best-selling relationship book or memoir or historical mystery. How do authors use those first five pages to draw in the reader? How do they pace their material so the middle doesn't "sag?" How do they use dialogue, anecdotes, or anything that you suspect isn't up to snuff in your manuscript?

Then find a professional, smart, supportive critique group, preferably with published authors, who can give you feedback and help you develop your work. As an added benefit, when you read and respond to their writing, you'll continue to develop your own skills.

Go to writing conferences and invest in professional critiques. Most conferences have opportunities for attendees to get feedback on their ideas or early pages. Take the plunge and sign up for a fifteen-minute appointment with an agent, editor, or published author, and ask questions.

And when you've done as much as you think you can, bring in the professionals. The expense of working with a professional book editor is often the first money you'll spend on marketing, and it's critical to success.[4]

For writers who are considering traditional publishing but haven't yet landed an agent or publisher, a professional editor can help you develop and polish your work, to help it stand out and grab attention from the very first page. If you're self publishing, hiring an editor is a necessity, not a luxury. *Do not skip this step.*

Finding the right editor is like finding the right contractor for your house: plenty of people are looking for your business, and only you can decide who best fits your needs. Without going into a ton of detail, here are a couple pieces of advice:

---

[4]To a certain extent, you get what you pay for. Shop around, compare prices, and ask for references. If an editing offer or service sounds too good to be true, it probably is. Plenty of scams are out there. (Unsure about an editor, agent, or publisher? Predators and Editors is a great resource: http://pred-ed.com/)

- Know what kind of editing you need: developmental (looking at the work's content as a whole and how successfully it's been developed), copy editing (ensuring style, accuracy, and consistency in the writing itself), or proofreading (usually the final step before publication, checking spelling, grammar, and formatting). Hiring someone to clean up your passive sentences when there are still major holes in the plot doesn't make your novel easier to market.

- Hire someone specific, with a professional editing background. Editing is a different skill than writing, and just because someone has written a few books doesn't mean that she or he knows how to evaluate another writer's work. As publishing houses downsize and the freelance market expands, it becomes easier to find editors with professional credentials and experience. Beware "editing" services from self-publishing or other author service companies that assign projects to anonymous editors. If you don't know the person's background, you don't know if he or she is qualified to comment on your work. Editing, like writing, is a subjective process. You could give your work to four different professional, fully qualified editors, and they might come back with four very different responses. It's up to you to find someone you trust, and whose vision for your work complements your own.

No book is ever "done," but when you're confident that you've taken it as far as possible, and then the professionals have helped you take it even further, and when you are confident that your book is comparable to or better than what else is out there, it's time to share it with the world.

Quality writing takes time, but you only have one chance to make that first impression. If you're ready to put your hard-earned time and money into promoting a book with your name on the cover, the absolute most important thing to do is to be sure that the final product is one worth promoting.

And when you know it is, then share it with pride.

Your turn

- How does your book stand up to the most popular books in its category? Be as honest as possible. If you're writing fiction or narrative nonfiction (memoir, some history), think about your characters, plot, conflict, dialogue, pacing, and resolution. (If you don't know what these words mean, then take a break and read a few books about writing craft.) In nonfiction, have you identified with the reader's felt need or point of curiosity and made a promise about how you will fulfill it? Do your chapters flow smoothly, building to a conclusion? Have you established yourself as a trustworthy narrator and included enough anecdotes and examples to make the book interesting?

- List three unique things you think your book has going for it, as far as writing goes. What do you hope that readers notice about your book? Its honesty? Its breakneck pacing? Its dialogue? Its evocative, emotional writing? Its clear message of hope for those who are suffering? Its original reporting?

- Ask your editor what he or she sees as the book's particular strength. What does she see as the thing that readers will want to talk about when they finish the book? (Your editor is a great person to give you a second opinion and to help you see your work in a new way.)

4

---

how high is your diving board?

"Audience development doesn't happen overnight (or even in 6 months or a year)—and it's a process that continues for as long as you want to have a readership. It shouldn't be delayed, postponed, or discounted for one minute." — Jane Friedman

"What you need to do is the hard work day by day in building a group of people who trust you, and want to support you when it's time." — Seth Godin

I F you've been hanging out at publishing conferences or in writers' circles, you've probably heard someone talking about platform. As in, "What's your author platform?" "Well, of course his book sold. Have you looked at his platform?" "Do you have enough of a platform to attract that agent/publisher?"

If you're already working with an agent or traditional publisher, you probably had to put together some kind of platform summary to help

calculate your first-year sales and profitability. Long before your book
has sold a single copy, you've had to quantify your relationships, round
up the counts of every person who attended a workshop or visited your
blog, and turn your reach into hard numbers. For some of you, that was
a cold and depressing process. For others, it was exciting to see how big
your communities have grown to be.

Or perhaps you haven't started to query agents and publishers, or
maybe you're self publishing and skipped the whole book proposal process. "Platform" might still be a mysterious word for you.

Don't let it stay that way. If you want to build an audience and
sell books, you need this intentional, well-maintained, and permanent
structure to help you rise above the crowd. And the best time to start it,
or to formalize it, is now—whenever "now" is for you.

One of the hard realities of publishing is that an author's marketing
efforts should start long before a book releases. It takes time to build your
name recognition, and an expensive advertising campaign or flashy book
jacket won't get you there. You need to build a day-by-day reputation as
a person to be trusted.

How does that work?

Your "platform" in publishing refers the collection of things you do,
steadily and over time, that help you build name recognition and trust
within your target audience. If, in my horribly extended metaphor, you
consider your audience as a pool of people, then your author platform is
the diving board that you're standing on to see them, and the higher it
is when you dive in, the more momentum you'll have when you hit the
water/release your book. (I did warn you about my need to overuse this
image...)

In today's hyperconnected world, there are dozens of ways for you
to communicate, share, and support your audience that go beyond—and
before—your book.

Marketing expert Seth Godin, author of *Tribes* and at least a dozen
other best-selling books, encourages aspiring authors to start building
their communities at least three years *before* their first books come out,
because it takes that long to build up the steady base of loyal followers
who will be early adopters and devoted ambassadors. If you launch a

platform at the same time you launch a book, it may not be tall enough for you to make a satisfying splash.

Those "overnight" success stories of writers who were "discovered?" When you look a little closer, you'll see that many of them had been building platforms for years. They're former journalists who decided to write a novel, or New York City natives who have been networking at literary events while accumulating rejection slips, or they're related to someone who once worked with someone else.

What if your book is already out, or on the verge of coming out? The good news is that you still have time to build a following. Your initial sales may not pay off the mortgage, but your book's not going anywhere, either. The digital age means that books don't go out of print. If you commit to a long-term strategy of building your platform, your book will still be there (perhaps joined by another title or two) when your audience is.

What's in a name?

It doesn't matter where your audience is or whether you connect with them online or in person. What does matter is that they know your name.

An author's name matters. You may not know what the latest title is from John Grisham or Stephanie Meyer or James Patterson, but it doesn't matter. You're drawn (or not drawn) to the name.

Consider the case of Robert Galbraith, a crime fiction writer whose first book, *The Cuckoo's Calling*, released in 2013. His bio indicated that Galbraith was a former plainclothes police officer and military veteran now working in private security. Several publishers considered the book but turned it down as "perfectly decent, but quiet," and nothing that stood out in the crowded crime genre.[1]

His early book sales were good by modern standards, though nothing spectacular: 8,500 copies across all English-language platforms (hard-

---

[1] Sam Marsden, "The Cuckoo's Calling: publishers' embarrassment at turning down JK Rowling detective novel," The Telegraph, July 14, 2013, http://www.telegraph.co.uk/culture/books/10178960/The-Cuckoos-Calling-publishers-embarrassment-at-turning-down-JK-Rowling-detective-novel.html.

cover, e-book, library, and audio) over its first three months of publication.[2] Then a friend of the publisher's lawyer leaked that Galbraith was a pen name for J. K. Rowling. In the next seven days, the book registered more than 17,000 new sales, and it kept growing from there.

It's not that *The Cuckoo's Calling* became a better book. It's that readers suddenly associated it with a name they recognized. The writing quality seemed more assured, the author's imagination more trustworthy. J. K. Rowling felt like an old friend. And while Robert Galbraith no longer had the military credentials that the fictionalized (with the publisher's permission) biography on the book jacket offered, he had something better: he had his readers' trust.

It's worth noting here that this author's name and reputation were primarily built on the books she wrote. Establishing your audience early is important, and a platform is critical to generate early sales and momentum. But the absolute, positive, *best* way for you to build your readership is to write another book, and then another after that. It's hard to build an income or a loyal readership with a single title. A second (and third, and fourth) book will reward their loyalty. So don't get so caught up in marketing that you forget to write.

However you set up your schedule—whether you can make this your full-time endeavor or need to fit it into the small corners of your life—spend at least half of your available Author Time writing the next book.

How are your numbers?

Nick was twenty-three years old when he wrote the proposal for his first book, a satirical guide for working at a nonprofit organization. There were a couple of warning flags that might turn off an agent: first, the author was young, which raises questions about whether he has enough experience to speak with authority. And second, the target audience of a niche of professionals was limiting. Were there enough people who cared about Nick's subject matter?

[2]Jill Lawless, "Rowling laments exposure of Robert Galbraith," Yahoo! News, July 24, 2013, http://news.yahoo.com/rowling-laments-exposure-robert-galbraith-153945642.html.

But instead of slipping into the circular "thanks, but no thanks" file, Nick's proposal generated a bidding war among publishers who were anxious for his book. Why? Because Nick had numbers.

- Three years: the length of time Nick had vlogging (video logging) on YouTube, sharing funny stories about his experiences and building a subscriber base of several thousand followers.

- Half a million—and counting: number of times Nick's most recent video for nonprofit workers, capturing the title idea for his book— had been shared. There were hundreds of positive comments, and when Nick shared his proposal the video was still viral and growing every day.

- Twenty: the number of high-profile nonprofit Executive Directors Nick had already approached about his ideas, who were willing to consider endorsing his book.

Nick used numbers to show publishers not only that there was an audience for his book, but also that he already knew how to reach them. His fans trusted him and would buy what he offered them. Publishers were welcome to come along for the ride.

Not everyone is Nick, of course. But everyone has the potential to build a network of trusting fans.

How many of your future readers already know your name and trust you as a voice in their community? (If you suspect that the answer is "not many," stick with me. The next chapter is all about how to increase this number.)

There are different ways to consider this. You can look at how many Facebook friends and Instagram followers you have—at least, you should count them if you're writing your social media profiles to appeal to your target audience. (If your Facebook friends are mostly your old high school glee club, and you're writing a legal thriller, it's harder to gauge how many will be interested.) You could see how many people are on your email newsletter list or compile a list of previous customers if your book is related to your existing business. Think about how many people attend the monthly professional meetup of social entrepreneurs that you help organize (if you're writing a book about changing the world), or how many folks are on your art installation team at Burning Man (if your project is a counterculture exploration that will appeal to burners). You've hopefully met other writers in your genre through your critique groups and writing conferences, or maybe you posted your writing online and built an early fan following. All these people will become your first buyers, your biggest supporters, and the ripples that push your impact out toward the pool's edges.

When it comes to platform, how big is big enough? This question comes up often, but there's no single answer. It depends on your genre, your competition, how you're publishing, and how you define success. The commitment rates of some audiences are higher than others. Your social media followers, for example, are typically less connected or committed to you than the people who intentionally signed up for your mailing list, and you'll convert fewer of the social media followers to become active book buyers.

And of course, one "Big Name" endorser is worth more than one person who attended a class with you two years ago. If you once saved Nicholas Sparks' schnauzer from a horrible swimming pool accident, and he promised to use all of his contacts to help you make your first book a success, then that might be your platform.[3]

Building trust takes time. Rowling had been publishing for fifteen years when *The Cuckoo's Calling* came out. You have to show an audience that you will consistently show up, time after time, with something worth saying.

Building your own platform

Building a platform sometimes happens organically. You may be an extrovert who is outgoing with your passions and public about your experiences. The same things that drove you to write have also pushed you to reach out to your target audience in other ways. You may be

---

[3]My legal counsel advises that I should point out here that I'm not advocating endangering dogs as a platform-building strategy. Some things must be left to chance.

reading this chapter and thinking, "Well sure, I have a couple thousand blog subscribers already."

If this is you, congratulations on being a natural marketer. Your new task will be to stay connected to the community, continue to grow your audience, and make sure you connect them back to your book.

For the rest of us (and I count myself among the introverts who are not natural networkers), building a platform needs to be more intentional. You've made the choice to be a published author, which means that on some level you've embraced, or at least accepted, the idea that you will be a public figure. People you've never met will know your name.

It's not enough to wait for readers to come to you. It's time to figure out how to go to them.

Start building a platform by taking an honest inventory of your strengths and abilities. Platforms are all shapes and sizes, and you need to figure out what best fits you and your audience. Where do they meet you? Why should they trust you?

Push past your love (or tolerance) of solitary book writing and think about how you best interact with the world around you. Do you have professional credentials and expertise in your subject area? Do you communicate better in formal writing, in groups, or in one-on-one relationships? How much time do you currently spend interacting online with people? Are you comfortable with public speaking (or could you get comfortable)? Do you love to research and share information? Do you have a strong visual eye for photographs or design? Are you a whiz at organization? In your spare time, do you goof off with a video camera? How much time do you spend reading books in your genre or researching your chosen subject?

If you're not good at these types of things now, what areas interest you, and what are you willing to commit time to developing?

At this point it's also a good idea to identify anything that you are absolutely uninterested in doing, or communication styles that fall well outside your skill set. Remember, marketing should be something that you potentially enjoy. There's no secret formula for book sales that says you have to do something specific. The only thing you *have* to do in book marketing is write a book; everything else should be considered an opportunity, not an obligation. If speaking in public terrifies you, or if you don't have the technology or interest in making videos, then cross those off your list. There are dozens of ways to build a platform, and you'll be more successful—and more trustworthy—if you don't hate what you're doing.

Once you've identified your strengths, the second step is to look at where those traits overlap with what you've already discovered about where your audience gathers. How can you meet them where they are?

If you're a natural connector who likes to hear about people's lives and share humorous quips about your own, and your audience spends a lot of time on Facebook, then you should be interacting (not just lurking) on Facebook. If your audience is seeking information, and you're comfortable providing it face to face, teach workshops. If humor is your thing, find a way to make people laugh. If your audience loves the blues, share music with them.

In the next chapter, we'll get specific with a few options and opportunities. For now, the important message is this:

Make yourself helpful.

Don't build a platform just to sell things to your audience. Build a platform because you value readers and have something to share. It may be your knowledge, your art, your service, or your questions. Whatever it's based on, your platform should be about giving, not getting. If you show up and talk only about yourself—your book and your goals and what you want—then your potential followers will quickly abandon you as a spammer. If you go into any of these and let your primary message be "I'm writing a book, and you should help me!" you will not develop a sense of trust.

And a platform that's not based on trust is a wobbly place to stand.

Your turn

- What do you want your future readers to think about when they hear your name? What is the reputation your platform will be built upon?

- What are you currently doing to maintain relationships and establish your platform? How many people are you currently reaching?

5

---

double pike or belly flop? choosing your own style

"Writers are like farmers: The harvest comes, but only after you toil for a few seasons." — *Cheryl Strayed*

"The more long-lasting connections you make with readers, the more books you will sell in a natural manner that reflects genuine connection rather than shady salesmanship." — *Tim Grahl*

Oкay, got it. We're here to build trust, share stuff, and make friends. That's all warm, fuzzy...and vague. You're a mystery novelist with a full-time job and a family. What does a platform look like in your life?

That's what Julie asked me. She'd landed a contract with a small publisher for her first book, a women's novel about a Southern family caught up in a legal battle over their adopted child, and she understood that most of the marketing would rest on her shoulders. Her book was a year from release, and she needed a platform that worked with her audience as well as her "day job," writing, and family. We explored various options and came up with a pre-release platform plan that helped launch her book into a crowded market (it's a tough sell when your competition is Jodi Picoult). I'll tell you more about the plan at the end of the chapter. First, let's talk about you.

Your opportunities to build a reputation are as diverse as the kinds of books and readers in the world. But when you're starting out, an answer like that isn't helpful. So here, as examples, are five popular ways that aspiring and new authors grow successful platforms. These all support book sales when you have a book to sell, but what sets these platforms apart is that they're primarily relationship builders, not sales channels. (No, you're not going to sell a lot of books through your Facebook page, but you're going to build relationships that eventually lead to sales.) These are long-term, audience-building commitments that will support you not just for your first book, but for your entire career.

Mix and match to find your perfect style, or use these as inspiration to build your own path. No one expects you to do all five. In fact, it's better if you choose, and really commit, to developing a couple at a time.

Each of these opportunities, on its own, could be the subject of a whole chapter, or even a whole book. But here's enough to get you started.

Publishing short pieces

Historically, writers built their credentials and honed their skills by publishing articles in magazines, short stories in literary journals, and even commentaries in newspapers. In those dark days before social media, publishing short pieces offered direct exposure to new audiences, and the two- or three-line bio at the end of a piece introduced readers to an author's website and previous publications.

We don't talk as much anymore about writing for other outlets, but all of those benefits above are still true. Essays in national publications, whether it's Salon.com or *Field & Stream*, can get your name in front of thousands of readers. And that list of your previous publications in your author bio adds credibility to your future work. Readers, as we've seen, trust writers with a track record.

If that was all you got from your articles and short stories, that may be enough to make writing for publications part of a pre-release platform. But something else makes publishing short pieces for your future audience even better:

It introduces you to the influencers who manage those outlets.

Influencers are the people who have gone into your chosen community before you and built substantial platforms of their own. They're magazine and journal editors, radio hosts, popular authors, respected book reviewers, bloggers, community managers, journalists, nonprofit organizations, businesses, and anyone else who has your readers' eyes and ears. Influencers matter, because building a relationship with a single influencer is often more valuable than acquiring a hundred average readers' names. (We call them "influencers," rather than "Important People," with the optimistic expectation that if they're approached correctly, influencers will be willing to share your project with their followers.) Every effective author platform is supported by a few influencers who can multiply a message and introduce it to even more people.

If you build a positive relationship with an editor, meeting his or her deadlines and showing that you understand the publication's audience and can relate to its issues, then you've earned the right to ask that editor to support your new book release down the road with a review, an endorsement, or other coverage. Most publications receive hundreds of books from publishers, publicists, and authors. It can be overwhelming (something I learned firsthand when I launched and ran a magazine for a few years in the early 2000s). Editors are more likely to cover books from authors they know.

Of course, publishing short pieces can be a time-consuming process. If you've never tackled article or short story writing, be prepared for a querying cycle that's similar to the traditional book-publishing process (but usually much faster). You need to identify the right channels for your work, pitch them on the story, and find time to write it. Every outlet, whether print or online, has submission guidelines, as well as its own voice and style. You'll need to do some homework to understand a publication's specific voice (Does it publish humor? Do the articles use a lot of statistics? Are its short stories all approximately the same length?).[1]

But the right story, at the right time, can expose your name and writing to thousands, or hundreds of thousands, at once. If you're most comfortable expanding your base through formal writing, this is a great way to build your reputation.

A different twist: Today, many writers are skipping the middlemen and directly building their audiences by self publishing their short works as e-books or sharing them online.

While my client Jack was editing and revising his spy thriller series, he built anticipation for his new blue-haired, counterculture heroine by writing two short (10,000 word) prequel stories that explored her back story and some of her early adventures. He published them as e-book exclusives on Kindle, and online readers were willing to take a chance on a new writer when the cost was only 99 cents. He sold a few hundred copies in the two months leading up to his "real" book launch, and those readers became his core audience, writing the first reviews and increasing his early sales numbers.

Is this the wave of the future? Perhaps for some. Bloggers have been directly publishing for their audiences for years (yes, online publishing is still publishing), bypassing the time and inconvenience of submissions and editors, and it's exciting to see that novelists now have similar channels. Producing your own short works means you can control the timing, skip the rejection cycles, and potentially even make a profit.

On the other hand, going solo means you miss out on building relationships with publishing influencers, the support of editors, and the exposure of another outlet's already-established readership. (It's not easy to get an article on *The Huffington Post*, but if you do, in one day your name and website will be seen by more people than most writers can reach through any other activity in a year.)

---

[1] Books like the Writer's Market or Novel & Short Story Writer's Market are good places to start to understand the scope and size of the journal and magazine markets.

A word of warning for this approach: if you e-publish shorts as a way to build your platform, do not skimp on quality. Your work should be professionally edited and formatted, and the cover should grab a browsing shopper's attention. If your e-book essay or short story is sloppy or unprofessional, if the writing is amateur or dull, readers will say so, and you will lose them.

Blogging

Ten years ago, blogging was the hot new thing. Everyone in publishing was enamored with immediate, personal, and trackable ways for writers to share directly with their audiences. Blogging was relatively user-friendly, didn't cost much or was free, and kept readers connected through the long, quiet periods between books. We all told a lot of writers that they had to blog if they wanted a book deal—and then we paid the price with thousands of horrible, boring blogs.

But blogging as a marketing tool is making a comeback. Most writers have figured out that blogs need to be more than a personal diary and that no one cares what you ate for dinner (that is, unless you're trying to build a community around food, and then people can't get enough of good food photos). As traditional media shrinks, readers have turned to bloggers to take up the slack. Readers trust and follow blogs that are topical and subjective, and that build communities around people with similar interests.

Writers who stay connected to their audiences through blogging understand one key fact: this is a regular, steady activity that grows over time and requires a steady commitment of time and content. Don't expect to build a fan base by writing one blog article. Your audience will come—and stay—when you've written hundreds. "Doing well with blogging," says Aaron Wall, author of the blog SEOBook.com, "is not about writing one key post, it is about performing day after day and helping a few people at a time."

Unsure what to blog about? Consider the explosion of book review blogs. As newspapers and print media cut back their arts budgets and laid off book reporters, readers desperate to sort through the abundant options started to blog about the books they read. Fans and followers started to show up, eager for recommendations and updates on new titles.

Book by book, these bloggers—often regular people with day jobs and families, who happen to like to talk about what they're reading—established themselves as influencers. It didn't take long before publicists caught on. Today, book bloggers are inundated with offers of free copies of books from publishers of all sizes in exchange for honest reviews.

Catch that? The average person who takes the time to make a website to track their book reviews is being sought out and courted by publishing houses—the very entities most aspiring authors would love to talk to. How much easier would it be to get the attention of a publishing house when you're already on a first-name basis with its publicity staff, and they already see you as an expert in the genre? And how much easier would it be to introduce your own novel to fans when they already trust your opinion on books?

So if you're a novelist writing steampunk mysteries, thinking about relevant ways to blog might be hard. Your everyday life in the Arizona desert doesn't have much in common with your heroine's adventures on a gritty, damp London street. However, you're regularly reading steampunk mysteries as a way to stay current in your field (because good writers regularly read their genre's new releases to understand the market). *That's* where you overlap. Write about the books you're reading.

Of course, a blog doesn't have to be about books. A blog can be about any subject that will interest your readers.

That last part is important. *A blog should not be about what interests you.* Your platform is about providing value to your audience. So what can you share on a regular basis that they will appreciate? What information, inspiration, or entertainment are they seeking? It might be art, information, or personal essays—whatever fits your voice and their needs. Here is an example of one author's blogging experience:

A novelist is developing a series of contemporary women's fiction novels set in the arid wine country of eastern Washington, where she lives. She blogs about things that happen in the region: the emerging wineries, the struggling ranchers, the history of the area. She regularly mentions her own writing process of trying to capture the region's dramatic landscape and unique personalities, but it's just one aspect of the way she experiences her community. She also writes personal stories based on her family's trip to the county fair, shares lots of beautiful photos, rates local restaurants, and reviews books that are set in the area. She attracts female readers who are interested in the area and who will be likely to read a book that is set there.

Or then there's the writer with three children who is working on a memoir about living with her infant's special needs. She writes a blog for other mothers of special needs children, linking to news articles about education and medical research, reviewing products that affect her family's life, and sharing stories about daily life with a special needs child. She attracts other families with special needs children, who will connect with her personal story and will want to read her memoir.

See the similarity? A blog written for your audience shouldn't become an opportunity to write exclusively about your own book or writing process. That kind of self-focused content may attract other writers who are interested in publishing, but it won't expand your reach to the people who will become fans of your crime thriller or history of paleo cooking.

Whatever you choose to write about, look for ways to make your posts, comments, and essays timely, focused, and short. (Ever try to read something on your phone that's 3,000 words long? It had better be a good article for me to do that much scrolling.) You don't need to blog every day; most writers don't have that much to say, and most readers don't want to make that kind of commitment. A blog that's updated once or twice a week, consistently and with quality content, is more valuable than something forced or rushed. And your blog should be easy to read; you should carefully proofread, but readers understand that your content will be less polished and more immediate.

Here's one more good example: a writer who was revising his crime thriller realized that he'd done a significant amount of research on the inner workings of courtrooms and police investigations. He watched the news differently, because he had new perspective about what was happening behind the scenes and knew that real investigations don't look much like what the media portrayed. So he created a blog that critiqued popular TV shows and movies, pointing out inaccuracies. He interviewed and profiled real crime-solving heroes, and over time attracted an audience who appreciated his role as an "amateur expert" source for understanding crime-related media.

Whatever you write about, include links to other websites, images, and other interactive pieces that help your readers expand their experience. Allow readers to comment on your posts, and be prepared to answer those comments and engage.

A different twist: Just because we're writers doesn't mean that our content must always be written. Remember Nick from the last chapter? He built his audience through a series of short, catchy videos that provided a tongue-in-cheek look at life inside the nonprofit world. If you're a visual person who's more comfortable with extemporaneous talking instead of writing or have a talent (drawing, knitting, motorcycle riding) that you your readers will enjoy seeing, you can also build your brand with a vlog.

Do you (or does someone close to you) have a web/video camera and some editing skill? Are you comfortable on camera, or are you willing to work to become so? Smart, well-made videos are easily shared online, and the best ones go viral, speeding across the Internet. If you want to try vlogging, create regular clips (one or two minutes is usually long enough) related to your area of expertise and your audience's interest. For example, if you're writing a memoir about your first year of urban farming, share video clips of the changing seasons and growing animals. If you're writing fantasy, create a series of video tutorials based on your research about sword fighting.

Social media: friends, fans, tweets, pins

Once the blogging fad passed, we publishing professionals turned our collective attention to social media. "Authors, go to Facebook and Twitter! That is where you shall find your audience and convince them to buy your book! You must have likes and followers! You must get retweeted by the right people! You must Pin and Instagram and Snapchat!"

The philosophy was right: don't make your readers come to you! Go to them! And stay in front of them!

But once again, we over-spoke. And millions (it seems) of well-intentioned writers flooded social media, where they were clearly uncomfortable, and they followed only one another (or they didn't bother to follow anyone), and they sent dozens of BUY MY BOOK messages (yes, in all caps) three times a day, which no one saw. They paid people to make Facebook pages for them, even though they'd never logged into Facebook before, and the pages sat, empty and neglected. They filled YouTube with awkward stock photos and sappy music and called them book trailers.

The backlash was expected. "Social media doesn't work," they said.

Well, no, not if you approach it that way.

Blasting your own sales-focused messages without engaging the community is like standing in the doorway of a crowded cocktail party shouting, "Buy my book!" and then slamming the door and running away before anyone responds. It's not only ineffective, but also rude.

What if you decided that, instead of signing up for another account and waiting for people to find it, you committed to being part of a community that happens to gather online, and you used the tools of that space to connect with people and to build stronger relationships with your readers and potential readers?

What if you *added value* to people's lives via social media?

Social media sites (the most popular arguably being Facebook, Twitter, Pinterest, Google+, LinkedIn, and Instagram) are valuable tools for writers to build communities and provide value. They're relatively easy to use, with templates and content management that doesn't require special technical knowledge or design skill. The audiences are already there. And the commitment to maintaining them is flexible enough to fit into the pockets of available time that every person has throughout the day. Once you get settled in and comfortable with a site, you can browse and comment on Pinterest while the coffee brews, or answer your Facebook messages while waiting to pick up the kids from school.

The important thing to remember, and the difference between a successful social media platform and one that flops, is that social media is meant to be *social*. Almost everything that's wrong about social media happens when authors treat their accounts as advertising channels, not social ones.[2]

For example, take George Takei's incredible social media platform. Best known for his role in the original Star Trek series and movies, Takei had maintained a steady presence in TV and films. But when he launched a Twitter account and Facebook page in 2011, his visibility exploded. At the end of the first year, he had 1.4 million fans on Facebook and 300,000 Twitter followers; by 2014 that number was up to 6.3 million on Facebook and more than 1 million on Twitter.[3] A whole new generation has discovered his voice, which he described in a *Forbes* interview as "a curious combination of geek/nerd humor and somewhat raunchy and irreverent banter."[4]

What's the secret? Takei has a great sense about what will make people laugh, and he uses it to draw an audience together and brighten their day, usually without asking for anything in return. He understands the power of visual images and shares pictures that stand out from the noise. And he posts every day, often more than once a day. He's not spending lots of time or money creating original content. Instead, Takei has become a master curator of jokes, photos, and memes—often found elsewhere on the Internet or shared by his fans and followers. He works in occasional commentary on the things he cares about—from LGBT issues to promotion of his own projects—but Takei described his purpose in the *Forbes* article as primarily fun, "combating idiocy with humor." The human tendency is to share what makes us happy. So his fans have re-posted, shared, retweeted, and become the megaphones that have launched his social media platform "where no man has gone before." (Sorry, couldn't resist.)

---

[2]The social media sites themselves can sometimes get confused about their purposes, and you'll get a fair amount of pressure from these sites to pay for promotions and ads. It's up to you to decide how important this is to your overall marketing effort, but it's worth noting that every survey and study of book buyers shows that advertising minimally influences their purchasing decisions. I wouldn't recommend paying for an ad or a post except in targeted, specific instances where you can attract new readers through a contest, event, or special offer. We'll talk more about advertising in chapter 7.

[3]https://www.facebook.com/georgehtakei and https://twitter.com/GeorgeTakei

[4]Alex Knapp, "How George Takei Conquered Facebook," Forbes, March 23, 2012, http://www.forbes.com/sites/alexknapp/2012/03/23/how-george-takei-conquered-facebook/.

Social media sites are constantly changing, and you don't need an account on every new site that pops up. Pay attention to where your readers and influencers are, and then *provide value* there.

So if you're not telling people to buy your book, what should you be doing? Whether you're writing in 140 characters or curating just the right Tumblr content, social media has many uses:

- *Educational or inspirational.* What's your platform built on? Are you providing information? If so, extend this to your social media site. Share links to articles that support your position, or create your own graphics to remind your followers what matters. Offer content that shows, over and over again, that you understand your audience, that you can answer their questions and solve their problems, and that they can trust you.

  Are you more inspirational? Is your purpose to brighten someone's day? Use social media to encourage your followers or make them laugh. Use funny pictures, motivational videos, or quirky takes on current events. Quotes—from famous people, from friends, from your own work in progress, or from your precocious two-year-old—are always popular.

  One of my favorite examples of Twitter success came from an author who wrote lighthearted women's fiction (what we used to call "chick lit") set on a horse farm in the weeks leading up to the Kentucky Derby. This author had been a horse trainer. When she got on Twitter, she was witty, funny, and very feminine, and she sought out others who had the same style. She scoured the Internet for photos of attractive men on horseback and shared them with the hashtag #hotriders. For the month leading up to the Kentucky Derby, each day she shared a photo of an outlandish hat worn at a past Derby. (Google Images is an amazing tool for easily finding pictures of outlandish things.) Her fans loved it and liberally "favorited" and retweeted. Mixed into the fun content, she also gave glimpses into her personal life—a funny thing that a waiter said to her or a cell phone photo of a splendid sunset—always in that same sharp, comedic tone that made her novels so much fun. Her audience grew quickly, and she regularly fielded questions on Twitter about her book and invitations to come speak at book clubs.

- *Megaphone.* The reason you've gone to these social media sites is because your audience is already there. So show off what else you're doing, and give your followers ways to further engage with you. If you're blogging, post links to your new articles (and occasionally go back and link to some of your older, still relevant pieces). If you have a guest article on another website, share the link. If you're speaking at an event or doing a bookstore signing, share the details and the registration site. Don't assume that your fans have gone to your website to find out what's new with you. Share it with them where they are.

- *Clubhouse.* Especially on community sites like Facebook and arguably Google+, recognize that your fans are already committed to you. Treat them as the friends and supporters they are. Give them timely updates, so they feel like part of your writing life. Did you finish a particularly difficult scene today? Did you send your manuscript to your writing group for final critique? Did a reviewer leave a great comment on your Amazon sales page? Use the space to offer "special features" and "behind-the-scenes" peeks, like the corner of a page of the new manuscript or an opportunity to vote on two options for the next book cover. Ask questions. The more you let your friends and followers know that they're special and that you appreciate them, the more they're going to support you.

And don't share only your own content. The idea of social engagement goes both ways. Respond to what others are sharing. Post notes of encouragement, congratulations, or sympathy. Recommend other writers, websites, or resources that your fans and followers might like. Years ago I worked with a writer who's since built a substantial online following. Every day, she posts a note of encouragement to someone in her community, and I'm lucky enough to still be in the rotation. It probably takes her ten seconds, but it makes my day every time to see something like

"@bethjusino is a great editor and I miss talking to her." I immediately want to share her words, and her books, with all my friends.

The 80/20 rule works well when you're thinking about social media: for every one message you post that might be considered self promotion (20%), post four (80%) that are purely to support your community and provide additional value.

If you're stuck for ideas, research other writers' pages and see how they communicate. What kind of links, encouragement, and inspiration are they sharing? What are their fans responding to?

However, be careful not to get too caught up in following everyone else's content. When I talk to writers who are getting started with social media, they're often overwhelmed by the constant flow of information that comes from friends, followers, connections, etc. How can you keep up with everything that everyone is saying? The answer is simple: you don't. Social media is like cable television—no one can keep up with all the different things that are broadcasting, and no one expects you to. Drop in when you can, and sample what's most recent.

What you should NOT do on social media sites:

- Try to advertise yourself. We've talked about this enough.

- Get controversial about off-topic subjects. If your platform is built on the importance of organic farming, then advocating for an anti-GMO bill makes sense. But if you write historical fiction, think twice before you go on that political rant against the president/senator/city council/local parking enforcement.

- Complain. Never, ever use your social media to criticize or complain about bad book reviews or negative experiences with your publisher/agent/publicist/local bookstore. If you're upset or emotional (or you've had one glass of wine too many), step away from the keyboard.

- Get careless. Like blogging, your fans and followers will accept a certain level of informality in your social media profiles. But you're a writer. For goodness' sake, check your spelling and punctuation.

A different twist: Whatever's newer and cooler than Instagram, Tumblr, and Pinterest. The world of social networks expands daily, with hot new sites emerging and fading with the cycles of the moon. Photo sites are trying to push Instagram off the photo sharing pedestal (just as Instagram pushed aside Flickr). YouTube's the biggest, but not the only, channel for videos of all sorts. A dozen new book communities are trying to take market share from Goodreads. If you find a new channel that appeals to you—*and you find your community there*—go to that site. Do your readers have their own social networking communities? Could you find them in a knitters' forum or on a steampunk photo-sharing site? Do they share stories and tips for tracing family trees in a genealogy network or review science fiction novels on a fan site? Don't overlook the potential of building your platform on smaller or lesser-known sites, which may be the best place to connect with a specific group and build their trust.

Volunteering for community and charitable groups

There are plenty of reasons to volunteer for groups that you care about, and most of them have nothing to do with book marketing. However, any time you're working with people who share your interests and fit your target reading audience (or who are influencers of that community), there's a platform angle to consider.

A few years ago, Janice was researching her first novel, in which the protagonist was fighting to protect a park on her island home. Janice's research led her to discover that recent state budget cuts had left actual parks in her state in danger of being sold. Concerned for the area's wellbeing, Janice volunteered for a community group that was trying to preserve the open space. She was eventually invited to sit on a statewide panel of nature conservation. This all unfolded over several years, while she was writing her novel. When it was ready for publication, Janice received endorsements from some of the most influential conservation advocates in the country, which opened the door for book marketing efforts (reviews, ads, interviews) in both regional and national conservation publications.

That's what can happen when your passion for a subject translates to a real-world platform.

This is a fine line to walk. I'm not advocating that you join a cause because doing so will help you sell some books. Authenticity matters here, and if you volunteer for your own selfish purposes, it will be obvious, and you will turn off the very people who could help you. However, it's important to talk about it here because introverted writers sometimes need a little shove to help them see the platform opportunities they're already engaged with. And taking your book ideas off the screen and into the real world will help your writing, adding depth to your understanding while building your audience.

Is there a charity or outreach program that's related to your book? If you're writing a memoir about a beloved pet, can you add to your research and build your passion for animal adoption by volunteering in a no-kill shelter? Could you volunteer at a fundraiser for youth literacy if you've written a series of children's books? Building homes for disadvantaged families when your novel's protagonist is a carpenter?

If you're stuck for ideas of where to get involved, look no further than your local writing conference. Hundreds of these events, large and small, happen across the country and around the world every year, and many bring a roster of successful authors, editors, and agents to teach workshops and mentor new writers. When you attend these events (yes, even after you've been published—most conferences have professional tracks for published writers) you have the opportunity to learn and to network. But if you take it a step further and let the organizers know that you'd like to *volunteer* at a writing conference, your opportunities multiply (and you may get a discount on the registration fee). You might be asked to be a guide or assistant to one of the high-profile speakers, giving you opportunities for one-on-one conversation. Or you might be assigned to man a registration table, usually with at least one other writer, with ample time for discussion and an introvert-proof reason to meet other writers and attendees.

Who can you meet, and what will you learn, when you're brave enough to step out and say "I'll help?"

A different twist: Rather than joining a group that's already established, some writers find that their passions drive them to create something that doesn't already exist. If there's not a group that's currently gathering and supporting your passion, maybe that's a sign that you're the person to start the nonprofit organization or organize your own event. If, for example, your passion is for hammered dulcimer music, and there's not currently a place for hammered dulcimer musicians in your area to share their music or learn from one another, maybe you're the person to start it.

Public speaking

And finally, let's talk about what happens when building an author plat-form means *actually standing on a platform*. Plenty of authors, especially in nonfiction, build their reputations and establish their expertise by speaking to groups.

You don't need to address conference halls with thousands of people or become the host of your own drive-time radio show to have a speaking platform. Build a platform a few names at a time by offering a regular class at your community center, church, or local college. Novelists and short story writers also can get immediate feedback on content and develop storytelling skills by participating in local open mic nights.[5]

Think about topics that you would feel comfortable speaking about and that would attract people in your area. How do those topics overlap with your author brand? If your book is about the importance of garden-ing for mental and emotional health, could you teach a class through a local hardware store about how to start a garden? If you have spent hours digging through genealogical records while researching your memoir, could you share a workshop through your local library to show attendees how to trace their own family trees?

Events often start small. Gradually, you'll find yourself speaking to larger rooms of people or being interviewed for larger audiences.

A different twist: Want to speak to an audience without the schedul-ing pressure of public speaking? Anyone with a laptop and a microphone

---

[5]See http://themoth.org, http://storynet.org, or Google "storytelling event" in your own city.

can build a speaking platform and attract an audience through podcasting. These Internet radio shows exist for every topic imaginable and are attracting niche audiences of like-minded, loyal fans. Podcasting is a time and technology commitment, but if you have an idea for a program that will appeal to your readers and the time to figure out the technical details of producing and distributing a program, set yourself up as a podcaster. Bonus platform points if you use your podcast to interview other writers and newsmakers who are going before you, and then building those connections with influencers for future endorsements.

Whatever you do, do this:

Remember, no one expects you to do everything that's listed in this chapter. Authors have used hundreds of different ways to build their platforms to reach their readers and create name recognition, and once you start mixing and matching, thousands of platform possibilities exist. All you need to worry about are the pieces that appeal to you and will help you provide value to your readers. You might commit to a weekly blog about your research topic and twenty minutes a day on Twitter to meet new people. Or maybe your preferred plan will be to create a monthly podcast that features new writers in your city (at the rate that new books come out, you'll never run out of guests), and you'll also volunteer for your local writing conference.

Whatever you choose to do, and whatever you most enjoy, make sure that you're tracking your platform with an email mailing list and that your audience is giving you permission to stay in touch with them.

"One way to sell a consumer something in the future," says Don Pepper in the foreword to Seth Godin's *Permission Marketing*, "is simply to get his or her permission in advance."

U.S. federal laws (the CAN-SPAM Act of 2003 being the best known) prohibit a business of any size (and you are a business) from sending unsolicited commercial messages. You can't take your Christmas card mailing list or your class roster from a workshop you gave in 2012 and send everyone on those lists an email to advertise your new book. Not only is it potentially illegal, but it's also annoying for the recipient to get a bulk mailing they never asked for—and the last thing you want to do is frustrate your future fans.

So be proactive. On your blog, Facebook page, and in any face-to-face opportunities you have, ask people to share their names and addresses, and appropriately contact them in the future about new releases, special events, and other writing-related news.

Do this even if you're building your platform and communicating with your fans regularly through social media. When you use a site like Facebook or Twitter, your contact lists are owned by someone else. If Facebook suddenly went out of business tomorrow, you'd lose your access to everyone who follows you that way. Would you have a backup way to stay in touch?

Do this even if you can't imagine having anything to share. It's better to have an address and not use it for a year than to find yourself on the brink of a book release and not have permission to share your news.[6]

Today newsletters are almost exclusively sent by email (sorry, postal service workers). Web-based services like MailChimp or Constant Contact can help you manage your list, design your newsletter, and take care of all the legal requirements for mass mailings (privacy, addresses, unsubscribe options).

How you use your mailing list will vary, depending on what you want to share and where you are in your publishing cycle. Be selective. No one wants to get a mass mailing every time you post to your blog or when a new review shows up on Amazon. Most authors find that a bimonthly or quarterly schedule works fine for general updates.

With a mailing list, follow the same rules that you developed for other platform tools. Concentrate on content that will interest your audience. That might include news about your books and events, but also look for ways to share resources that may be of interest to your readers, such as links to articles, photos, recipes, or tips.

And don't get discouraged when the audience doesn't immediately appear. You may blog for only ten readers the first few months. Your first

---

[6]Unlike a certain book marketing expert you may know, who for years has told writers to build their mailing lists but failed to set up her own until a few weeks before her first book released. Even experts make mistakes... (which reminds me—you can now sign up for my shiny new email distribution list at http://bethjusino.com).

newsletter might have only twelve names. But as you find your voice and start to expand your audience, those numbers will grow. And with that, your loyal reader base that will support your books will also grow.

Remember Julie, from the beginning of the chapter? She and I worked together to build a platform plan for her that started a year before her first novel released. Julie understood that she had two important things going for her: first, she'd been an active part of her local RWA (Romance Writers of America) chapter and their online discussion forums for several years while she was learning the craft of writing. And second, as a licensed family counselor, she had a lot to say about parent-child dynamics— material that had inspired her novel but went much further. So Julie invested in a website and started a blog, where twice a week she wrote about how families handle crises. She reacted to true-life events in the news, highlighted interesting research she'd found while she was writing, curated advice she found elsewhere on the Internet, and shared pieces of her own story, both as an adopted child and an adoptive mother. Visitors to the site found both information and inspiration. (And of course, she encouraged people who visited her website to sign up for her newsletter, so she could let them know when her book released.)

Once the site was up and running, Julie started to share links to her articles with her RWA group, explaining how her research could help other novelists develop their own stories and characters. She continued to comment and connect on other subjects across the forums, and she volunteered to be a speaker's assistant at the next regional convention. The writers she met, online and in person, started to read her blog and shared it with their own fans and followers. A few published authors offered to read Julie's new book and write endorsements. One was con- nected to a popular association of book clubs, and they picked up Julie's book as a recommended selection. That pushed her early sales, and Julie's gone on to get contracts with a bigger publisher for three more books. She keeps blogging and supporting other Southern writers, and her sales keep growing.

That's what a platform based on trust and value can do.

Your turn

- What, if any, current channels are you investing in to build your platform? Are you enjoying them? Why or why not?

- If you're not currently growing a platform, or if you find yourself miserable in your current platform choices and in need of a "do over," what new project or projects will you take on to expand your platform over the next year?

- What are your goals for your platform? Don't try to measure the potential audience size. Instead, measure what you can control. Some examples of platform goals include the following: "I will identify and schedule at least six local speaking engagements this year." "I will blog twice a week for the next nine months." "I will volunteer at this year's local writing conference and introduce myself to at least ten people who inspire me."

part two

ACTive marketing (aka the book launch)

In which I abandon the overused swimming metaphor in favor of a borrowed acronym, in order to present you with specific, practical, short-term projects that can promote a new book release.

part two

ActiveMarketing
(and the book
launch)

6

---

making your book
A-C-T for itself

"If you can't judge a book by its cover, then someone's not doing their job." — *Anonymous*

B Y this point, you're building a platform, or planning to build a platform, or at least you can no longer claim not to know what a platform is and why it's important. You've edited and revised and polished and checked your book for the one thousandth time. And now it's here: it's time for the book release.

Watch out, sharks—you're about to join the feeding frenzy.

The shift from aspiring, platform-building writer to published, book-selling author opens a whole new set of marketing opportunities. Once the book is out, you're not only counting people in your audience, you're also tracking actual book sales. The pressure's on.

A book can be promoted hundreds of ways, from advertising to book club appearances, sale prices to blog tours. Thousands (or so it seems) of opinions exist regarding which ones "work." And there's only one of you.

Who has time to enjoy any of this?

You will, if you remember that you don't need to chase every fad, and you don't need to do it all at once. The first few months of a book release may feel like a sprint, but they're still part of the overall book marketing marathon.

If you're working with a publisher, your first priority in promoting a new release should be to make sure that you have open, positive communication with the marketing team, so that you can coordinate efforts (or at least not step on each other's toes). Most of the packaging decisions, like cover design and pricing, will be things that they handle. But don't wait for them to come to you with ideas. Ask if they will be featuring the book at any specific conventions or events, and offer to join the sales team for book signings or appearances, if it's appropriate. *And let them know what you're planning.*

The more your publisher knows about your personal marketing strategy, the more they can support you (and the more enthusiasm you might be able to build in-house; when a publisher knows that an author is committed to promoting his or her book, that usually motivates them to invest more of their own time and resources). Be sure to tell your publisher about speaking engagements, local media appearances, special launch parties or contests, or any other unique programs that you're putting together, especially in the first 3-6 months after release.[1]

If you're self publishing, your challenge is to get organized and stay organized. Creating and launching a book can feel like a full-time job, and the more you have lined up in advance, the better. You'll need to set aside a chunk of time every day, or at least every week, to tackle the marketing roles of both author and publisher.

So what are these marketing ideas that need to be organized and communicated? I'm glad you asked.

---

[1] A word about working with the publisher's marketing team: as an author, you have one new book to promote, probably for at least a year. This is the center of your world. But your publisher has multiple titles releasing that season, and in 3-6 months they'll have to move on to the next set of releases. This isn't personal, so don't take it that way. Be both gracious and persistent in working with them (one author friend calls her attitude "don't be a doormat, don't be a diva"). Clearly communicate how you plan to promote your book, and ask them to share their plans and activities, so you can be supportive. But don't give your publisher a list of things that you expect them to do to promote you, or take it personally if they plan less than you hoped for.

The A-C-T approach

There's no formula to sales success. If there were, then we could make every book a bestseller.[2] But certain strategies will help you wade through the opportunities to identify the pieces that complement one another and provide potential book buyers with every opportunity to support your writing.

In 2010, Shama Kabani wrote a book called *The Zen of Social Media Marketing*.[3] In it, she introduced a simple approach that I latched onto, because it applies far beyond social media.

Normally, I'm not a fan of acronyms and all their catchy, businessy cheesiness (SWOT, anyone?), but I'll make an exception for this one, because it's not a random string of letters—it's a reminder to authors that book sales don't just happen. Readers don't discover new books in a void.

Fostering positive impressions requires active effort.

And so an author's marketing plan has got to A-C-T: Attract, Convert, and Transform the customer.

Attracting is bringing new eyeballs to your book. This step is about simply building awareness, and getting your name and book title in front of people you don't know, in a positive way they will remember. Attraction is all about that first impression, and in those first moments of contact, there's almost never a direct "buy me" message.

Converting is the step in marketing that turns an *attracted* stranger into a customer (purchaser of your book) or a consumer (part of your platform audience, someone who subscribes to your newsletter, follows you on a social media channel, or otherwise agrees to "keep in touch"). While the ultimate goal is to convert them to customers and sell more books, don't discount their roles as consumers. Committing to you by sharing their name, address, or time is an enormous first step into developing a fan.

---

[2] Don't think too hard about that sentence. If every book was a "best" seller, then what is it better than? Oh, never mind.

[3] The entire updated and expanded edition is worth checking out and goes into extensive detail about effective ways to build an audience in social media: The Zen of Social Media Marketing: An Easier Way to Build Credibility, Generate Buzz, and Increase Revenue by Shama Kabani, BenBella Books, 2013.

Human beings are motivated by a concept called social proof: if we think that other people are doing or enjoying something, we're more likely to try it, too. So the final part of the A-C-T marketing approach is **transforming**, sharing past and present successes (in this case, positive reader experiences and public recognition) as a way to attract even more sales and fans. After all, one person who buys a book is great. One person who reads a book, loves it, and tells twenty of his or her friends (with or without your help), is even better.

Everything you do to promote your book must cover at least one of the three A-C-T steps. A solid marketing plan balances its efforts to cover all three.

To show you what that looks like in practical terms, let's look at how A-C-T affects your primary sales tool, your book package.

Because forget what they told you in middle school. Looks do matter. You can have thousands of social media followers and a great advertising campaign, but if readers aren't drawn to the book itself, you'll have trouble making a sale.

Attract

With your book, the cover design makes the first impression. And that impression is made ridiculously fast: according to a statistic thrown around often in publishing circles, the average book browser (online or in person) spends *eight seconds* considering a book cover before making a purchase decision.

What impression does your book cover give in eight seconds?

"Our brains are wired to process images faster than words," says Mark Coker, author and founder of the e-book publishing engine Smashwords. "When we see an image, it makes us feel something."[4]

Or at least it should. A good book cover design instantly tells the reader whether your book is whimsical or authoritative, whether it's an adrenaline-pumped ride or a lighthearted adventure.

---

[4]Terri Giuliano Long, "Yes, We Really Do Judge Books by Their Covers," IndieReader, May 29, 2013, http://indiereader.com/2013/05/yes-we-really-do-judge-books-by-their-covers/.

It should be built with layers of images, text, and white space (which, designers tell me, isn't always white). I can't explain much about the mysteries of how it all works; as a person without a lot of visual sense, I understand that book covers deliver an impression in both an emotional and a rational way, but I don't know exactly how that happens. I know that contrasting colors draw the eye, but I don't know how to choose the right shades.

But even I know when a cover is bad. When the font is hard to read, the photo is sloppily edited, or the proportions are off, the book whispers that it wasn't held to high standards. When a cover is too busy, too plain, or somehow just wrong, it pushes browsers away.

One book reviewer says that she looks at the covers of every book pitched to her. If the cover is bad or "cheap looking," she says in the *IndieReader* article, "'I wonder what other areas lack quality and refinement.'"

We do judge books by their covers, which is why cover design is not something amateurs should undertake. Unless you have a background in design and art, please don't try to design your cover yourself, or insist that the professional designer you or your publisher is paying use the photograph that your husband shot on vacation last year, or the illustrations of your story that your twelve-year-old niece drew.

If you're working with a traditional publisher, they will hire an artist to create the cover image. Your job as the author is twofold: first, to provide as much information and context as possible about the content, audience, and emotional connection; and second, to communicate clearly and calmly if the initial design doesn't fit the book. Most cover artists don't read the entire manuscripts of every book they work on, so they count on you to communicate what's important.

If you are self publishing, this is the time to put your money on the table and invest in a professional designer who has experience working in your genre. This is not a place to skimp or rush—if the cover doesn't attract readers, they'll never read your work. Look at the designer's previous book covers. Without knowing anything about the books, would you buy them, based on the first impression?

If that's impossible, and you can't afford a few hundred dollars for an original design, the Internet has you covered. You can buy a professionally designed stock cover for less than it costs for a dinner out, and some self-publishing sites even provide stock covers for free. It may not be entirely unique—other authors may buy the same package and use the same image or layout—but at least the cover will be pleasing to the eye and make a good first impression.[5]

Not sure how to choose a cover design? Try asking strangers in a bookstore, library, or other place where your target audience gathers. Show them a mockup (or two or three different ideas) and ask, "Would you buy this book? Why or why not?" Don't introduce yourself as the author, or you'll bias their responses; most people will avoid the truth if they think it will hurt your feelings. And don't ask, "Do you like this cover?" It's easy to *like* something but harder to commit to buying it.

Convert

Studies show that once a cover design draws a book browser in, the jacket copy makes them commit. This short description (used on the back cover or inside flap of the physical book, and the product description on the online retail sites) is your best chance to make a reader want to open the book and find out more.

Don't put it off until the last minute or ignore it completely.

Well-written cover copy gets to the heart of the book in 100-200 words, so every word and sentence needs to be there for a reason. If you're traditionally publishing, your acquisitions editor or marketing team will provide the description. In most cases they'll show it to you before it's finalized, so you can work with them to make sure it captures the right spirit and information. (If you think you're being left out of the loop, but it's not impolite to ask to see the copy before it's finalized.) If you're self publishing, you can write your own copy, or if you don't have

---

[5]The details of cost and vendors change too often for me to commit them to a book. I've got an up-to-date list of recommended sites and vendors on my website, http://bethjusino.com.

an advertising or copywriting background, hire a professional to write it for you.

In nonfiction that's written to teach or inform (what's called "prescriptive nonfiction"), effective cover copy is about what the reader will get from the book. It identifies with the reader's need (which we covered back in chapter 3), and then promises that the book will meet that need or solve the problem.

In fiction, effective cover copy introduces the major character (or characters) and the *inciting incident*: what happens that sends Our Hero into the state of physical or emotional instability, which she will spend the rest of the book trying to resolve?

Either way, don't try to summarize the whole book. When I'm writing copy for clients, I try to never give away details that happen after the first 50 pages. If your book offers a six-step process to a healthier gallbladder, don't try to list all six steps. If you're writing a memoir or biography, don't describe all the major scenes or turning points. Cover copy is a teaser; if you give them too much right away, the reader has no reason to open the book.

For example, say you've written a young adult novel about a teacher's-pet high school student in Arizona, who discovers that her chemistry partner is about to cut school to go rescue his family members, who are Mexican nationals smuggled over the border by corrupt coyotes and then abandoned in a storage unit two hundred miles away. The cover copy needs to give enough information to make the character unique (not just "a 15-year-old," but "Ella, a 15-year-old honor student who's never been in trouble or done anything that would get her in trouble"), and the description of the conflict should describe what's at stake ("now she must decide what to do: should she go with him to help, breaking the law and putting her own future at stake? Or should she let him face the dangerous border town alone, putting his life at greater risk?"). Stop there. Don't try to tell the reader what Ella decides or what adventures she and her lab partner get into along the way. To get that kind of detail, they have to read the book.

Transform

Have you ever wondered if those quotes and reviews printed on a book jacket impact sales? Well, I can answer with a confident "probably." Most readers don't admit, "I bought this book because there's a quote from Stephen Colbert on the front saying that I should." However, a quote from Stephen Colbert, or *Publishers Weekly*, or some "bestselling" mystery author you've never heard of, does seem to work in a buyer's subconscious to reassure her that an expert she trusts (or assumes she should trust) has read the book and promises it doesn't suck. A strong review or endorsement also influences bookstore and library decision-makers when they're considering what to add to their shelves.

That's what transformation is all about. Those extra words on a book's back cover or first pages that say, "This is the best book I ever read!" and "Twelve thumbs up!" add credibility and speak to our need for social proof.

To get an endorsement or review for your book's jacket copy, you'll need a finished (or almost finished) manuscript several months prior to publication. Don't rush into this. Unless you have a close relationship with a potential endorser, don't ask him or her to read a manuscript that's still rough or unedited. If you're going to ask people to lend their names to your work, you want them to see how great you can be.

There are three different kinds of endorsements:

Prepublication reviews. For decades, a handful of well-known magazines and publishing groups, collectively called "the trades," have reviewed prepublication books and offered their opinions on what's worth paying attention to. Getting a good prerelease review from *Publishers Weekly*, *Kirkus Reviews*, or a genre-specific outlet like *Romantic Times*, can create an early buzz among professionals (because let's face it, the average reader doesn't read *Library Journal*) as well as a respectable quote to excerpt on the book jacket.

If you're working with a publisher, they will handle soliciting reviews from these outlets. If you're self publishing, the opportunities for trade reviews are limited. At this point, most traditional publications only consider self-published books under separate imprints and programs—

Publishers Weekly's BookLife, *Kirkus Indie, ForeWord's* Clarion Reviews, etc.—that charge for their services.[6] Some outlets still refuse to consider self-published books at all. But the good news is that the self-publishing review services will consider a book after it has been published, which isn't true for their free, selective programs for traditional publishers. There's no need to delay your release for months just for the sake of a blurb.

Influencers. Most quotes you see on book covers come from other published authors or celebrities, who lend their names and "blurbs" to a new work. (Nonfiction books that open with forewords—longer endorsements written by an influencer or expert other than the author—fall into this same category.)

Whether or not you have a traditional publisher, the transformative marketing work of gathering endorsements from authors and influencers is almost always an author's job. That's because most influencers are hesitant to lend their names to anyone other than a writer they already know. (Another reason why you should be establishing a platform and making connections with influencers in your field before you publish.)

Be strategic about who you approach for an early printed endorsement. Some of your influencers may not have national name recognition (perhaps they're the CEO of a company, the pastor of a church, or a local media personality), or their platform extends in a different direction than your audience (you wrote a science fiction novel, and your influencer is a

---

[6]There's some controversy in the publishing world over whether you should pay for a review. You need to follow your conscience, but my take is that not all reviewers are created equal. The established publications, which only read and reviewed a few of the hundreds of traditionally published books they received every week, weren't equipped for the time or financial costs associated with opening their doors to a flood of self-published books, or for the dramatically different quality levels that result from publishing without gatekeepers. (Yes, there are brilliant, professional, edited self-published books, and you probably wrote one of them. But no matter how much you defend self publishing, let's face it: thousands of people didn't write books with that kind of quality.) Charging for submission was a way—perhaps a temporary way, and there are already signs that it's changing—to try to limit the number of submissions to those who were serious about getting the reviewers' attention and to recoup some costs associated with considering those submissions. But the offer comes with a guaranteed professional, unbiased opinion. Just because you're paying for someone to read it, don't expect that person to say kind things if your book doesn't meet industry standards. On the other hand, numerous online scam sites will sell you a few paragraphs of generic praise and say you can use their "review" in your marketing materials. Those companies haven't built reputations of honesty or quality, and their opinions aren't worth the money you pay for them.

personal trainer who wrote a business book). In these situations, having their name on your cover won't bring the kind of transformative sales effect you want. Save these contacts, and find other ways to connect with their audiences after the book debuts.

Give your endorsers a firm deadline for when you'll need their feedback in order to include quotes on the book itself, but if he or she can't commit to the timeline, welcome an endorsement whenever and however you get it. You can always add a blurb to your website and other marketing materials.

If this section is making you panic because you already published or are on the verge of publishing and don't know any authors who might endorse your book on short notice, don't worry. Blurbs aren't required. As your book gains readers and you put some of the other marketing ideas presented into practice, your circle of influential contacts will grow.

Readers. Remember "iluvbunnies21" from chapter 3? Well, if that online reviewer absolutely LOVED a book (why is it always in ALL CAPS?), some authors and publishers will say so on the book cover. Instead of soliciting "big" names or publications (or maybe in cases where influencers or trade reviews weren't available), the blurbs look something like:

> *Readers agree:*
>
> *"I couldn't put it down!"*
>
> *"I was up until 4 a.m., and it was worth every minute of missed sleep!"*

This is a judgment call. In the era of Yelp and Goodreads, when the opinion of "Amber M" carries as much weight with our restaurant choice as a Zagat review, there's a nice sense of democracy to honoring the readers who appreciate your work. But without verifiable names, this kind of endorsement is suspiciously easy to fabricate and may not bear much weight with readers.

If a recognizable name will say that your book is worth reading, go with that.

And there you have it. In a package of 6 x 9 inches (or smaller), you've managed to Attract, Convert, and Transform a book browser and hopefully have made another sale.

But what about the people who aren't browsing for books? How do you get your book in front of the readers who aren't looking for it, and how do you convince them to buy it? Over the next three chapters, we're going to dig more deeply into these ideas of Attract, Convert, and Transform, and how you can A-C-T to support each goal.

(Okay, I admit it: there's still something cheesy about the acronym. But we're committed now.)

Your turn

- Go to a bookstore (real or online) and consider at least 20 recently published books in your genre. What similar aspects do you see in their cover designs (art, layout, font, title, and subtitle)? Do these elements belongs on your book cover?

- While you're browsing, read the cover descriptions of 10 different books. Do the descriptions make you want to read the books? Why or why not?

- How does your own book package (cover design, copy, endorsements) stand up to the competition? Does it Attract, Convert, and Transform the reader's experience?

7

---

who are you again?
attracting readers

"We don't know where our first impressions come from or pre-cisely what they mean, so we don't always appreciate their fragility." — *Malcolm Gladwell,* Blink: The Power of Thinking Without Thinking

There are seven billion people in the world. There are twelve million books on Amazon. There is one of you. How will the right readers find you?

That, in a nutshell, is what Attraction marketing is all about—getting you and your book visible, and making a positive impression while you do it.

If you're a new author and haven't already spent years building your platform and cultivating your reputation, pay extra attention to the ideas in this chapter, because you'll need to spend the bulk of your time raising your visibility and making people aware of your book. After all, if they don't know about it, they can't buy it.

There are dozens of ways to attract readers to a new book release, and the best strategies incorporate a variety of efforts, spread over time, that complement what you're already doing with your platform.

Catch that? You need more than one Attraction effort to bring in enough readers to sustain the attention you need. Most marketing research says that a potential buyer needs to be exposed to a name or product as many as six times before they make a commitment. A profile article in a newspaper may expose you to a few thousand people and lead to a few dozen sales. That's fantastic. But tomorrow that newspaper is in the recycling bin, and those readers have moved on to an article about repairing potholes. If you want your sales to continue, you'll need to show up in front of a new community next week, and the week after that, until you've achieved enough momentum to carry your book forward. (This is where having a steady, active platform already in place before the book launches will help.)

To get started, choose a few specific projects from this list, or use them as inspiration to help you develop your own Attracting ideas.

1. Press release #1

For a lot of the authors I've met, media coverage is the ultimate sign of a successful book release. Press coverage definitely succeeds in Attracting new readers. A well-placed article or interview, especially in national media, will expand your reach. And let's be honest: being interviewed or profiled by someone "famous" is exciting.

But before you shell out a lot of money to a publicist who promises that they have a connection at *The Today Show*, think carefully about the story you're trying to pitch. There's not much of a news hook in "new, not-yet-famous author releases book." That happens almost 1,500 times a day.

You'll need a better angle if you want to draw the media's attention. Reporters, bloggers, and TV show booking agents are looking for a timely story that only you can tell, or a piece of information or advice that will benefit their audience. Make that press release about something more than just another new book. For instance, consider these ideas:

- Can you connect yourself or your book to current events, local news, or a popular human-interest story? Instead of trying to catch a reporter's attention with a piece that's all about your book release, offer to be an expert on something that's already happening, bringing your own unique perspective.

For example, not long ago I worked with a Hispanic woman who writes science fiction—an unusual combination. Her new book would release in August, a few weeks before National Hispanic Heritage Awareness Month.[1] So we developed a press release and media kit that focused on her personal story, rather than her book, and pitched her as a great resource or human interest interview to tie into the month of coverage. The author's local media responded to the idea, and not only did she land several interviews for TV and radio, but she also was invited to attend a special city-wide luncheon for Hispanic women, where she connected with journalists and influencers she could contact in the future.

Another novelist took a creative approach to land newspaper, radio, and five separate TV appearances for her fantasy novel (not the type of book usually covered on the evening news). She did it by "newsjacking," which is the term for when a writer or publicist responds quickly to breaking news and finds a way to insert their own story into the larger one.[2] In this case, the author—who happened to have an advanced degree in medieval history—sent a press release to local media on the eve of the much-talked-about season premiere of the TV show *Game of Thrones*, offering to comment on the accuracy of the show to the time period. In each interview she mentioned how her research had influenced her own writing, and made sure that the interviewer included the name of her book. Just like that, her novel was being talked about in the same sentences as one of the most popular shows on television.

---

[1] Whether you're writing about puppies or prostate disease, Congress has probably set aside some time to honor it. If you're considering a press campaign, Google around to find out if a relevant holiday exists that you can use as an intro.

[2] Newsjacking is a great marketing strategy that you can use not just in press releases, but across your content channels. Check out the book *Newsjacking: How to Inject your Ideas into a Breaking News Story and Generate Tons of Media Coverage* by David Meerman Scott for more information.

- Do you have an upcoming event? If so, invite local print, TV, and radio reporters. Gatherings make great human-interest stories, especially if they're tied to a charity (see #3 below), a holiday, or have something that looks great in pictures (Costumes? Props?).

With media outreach, most authors think they have to hire a publicist. And if you have a big enough story (and a big enough budget), a good publicist will bring you professional experience and established connections with relevant journalists. However, publicists are expensive—possibly the single most expensive thing that you'll do in marketing—and they can't guarantee that their efforts will bring results. Weigh the potential, immeasurable benefits that you'll get from media exposure against the cost. Choose your publicist carefully. Just because someone says they can promote you doesn't mean that they can. Ask for references and examples of their successful past campaigns. Have they had success with authors whose audiences and platforms are similar to yours?

If you don't have a book or story with national appeal, or if a publicist is outside your budget, you can manage your own local media campaign with a little creativity, research, and the Internet. Dozens of online tutorials show how to write a basic press release, or you can hire a copywriter to put the release together. Most news outlets have a "tips" or "submission" address posted on their websites. Start local—newspapers, TV, and radio—with your story pitch, and see if the opportunity grows from there. Websites like Help a Reporter Out[3] also connect journalists who are already working on stories with willing subject matter experts— like you—who are eager to be interviewed.

2. Press release #2

Not all news is shared through traditional media though, and some private outlets will love to get that "Author Releases New Book" press release—especially if the outlet has some relationship with you or a vested interest in sharing your personal successes.

---

[3] http://www.helpareporter.com

Does your alma mater, your place of worship, or your employer have a regular publication for members or employees? Does your neighborhood have its own local blog, or does the free newspaper at the grocery store have a place for community updates? This is low-hanging fruit. Email them an announcement about your new book release, preferably with an image of the book cover. Small organizations are often eager for content and are happy to celebrate with a hometown hero.

3. Donations and charitable relationships

We've already talked about how volunteering your time for a charitable cause, religious group, or other community-based entity might help you build a platform—and how this is a tool to use for good (helping the charity, supporting the cause) and not for evil. Whether you took up the challenge as part of your platform building or not, having a book in hand gives you more opportunities to do good and to gather new followers in the meantime.

If you have a passion for a charitable organization or group, especially if it connects somehow to the message of your book, you can donate a percentage of the proceeds and/or include a page of information about the group with your material in the back of the book, encouraging readers to get involved on their own. You can also donate autographed books to a group's library, put together gift baskets for silent auctions and fundraisers, make special appearances at donor events, and generally do whatever you can to use your work to bring additional attention to a cause you support.

So how is this marketing? Because it exposes you and your work to their audience. Charities may profile supportive authors in their annual reports and newsletters as an example for other potential donors. Schools might invite authors to speak at their fundraising events, especially if they have used the author's book as donor gifts.

None of this is a guaranteed result—the response you get will depend on the organization's size and needs, and the appropriateness of the book to the audience. But if you see a possible overlap between an organization's audience and your own, it's worth pursuing. The worst thing that will happen is that you'll do some good for a worthy cause.

4. Sharing promotional material

For years you toiled in obscurity, writing a book that only you, your critique group, and your editor read. But now you're a published author, and once that news gets out the most unexpected people, from the grocery store bagger to your OB-GYN, will ask about your book.[4] Get comfortable with your two or three sentence description of yourself and your work. ("I'm a writer for new moms. I have a memoir out about our crazy first year of parenting, and I'm working on a snarky collection that parodies all of those inspirational daily thought books.")

But don't expect anyone to remember what you tell them.

It's not personal, really. These are all potential readers (or the mothers/sisters/uncles/friends of potential readers), but they're also busy. Even those with the best intentions will go home and get distracted on the way to the computer by the cat throwing up on the carpet or the kids needing homework help. By the time they're done, they vaguely remember that they met someone who wrote something, but what was it?

And not only that, but your enthusiastic friends, family, and those influencers you've been courting might ask how to get the word out about your title. It's wise to have a simple visual reminder, like postcards or bookmarks, that include your book cover image, a tag line or marketing hook that describes the work, and ordering information. Every promo piece should also have your author website address, so curious readers can find out more. (We'll talk more about websites in chapter 8.) Postcards or bookmarks are also good to have on hand at conferences, writing groups, and even coffee shops, where there might be table displays to announce member news.

---

[4] That is, they will if you tell people the truth when they ask, "What do you do?" Some authors choose to write under a pen name and keep their publishing separate from their everyday lives, but when you're a new author trying to launch a career, this seems like a wasted opportunity (unless, of course, your writing might negatively affect your "regular" life; if you're a kindergarten teacher writing erotica on the side, you should avoid handing out postcards in class).

These are like business cards for your book. Your publisher may be able to design and print some for you, but if not, they're relatively inexpensive to order online.

Share them liberally with everyone you meet, from the waitress in a restaurant to your local librarian. One author I know always tips service people (waitresses, baristas, car mechanics, etc.) well, and she always gives them a bookmark with her book information. It's not unusual for her to return to a restaurant several months later to hear that the waitress bought copies of her books, and now she's telling her friends about them.

That's building the fan base, one person at a time.

5. Throwing a great launch party

If parties are your thing and you have a dedicated community of friends and family, draw attention by launching your book in style—and in person.

A launch party is a celebration of your months and years of hard work, and it's a way for you to both thank the intimate community that supported you and to create a stir that attracts new fans and followers. For a marketing-savvy launch party, you should invite everyone you know and choose a venue that's appropriate for your content. That might be a local bookstore (tied in to a book signing, something else we'll talk about in chapter 8), but a different, creative place in your community might provide a memorable experience for your readers. (A science museum for science fiction? A tea shop for a cozy mystery?) Provide appropriate refreshments and fun book-related activities (quizzes, costumes, photo booths, icebreakers) to help your guests mingle.

Most launch parties include a short (emphasis on *short*—no more than five minutes) reading of your favorite part of the work. Have plenty of copies of your new release on hand to sign for guests. Book sales can be handled in plenty of ways: invite a bookstore to come and sell copies on site, give copies away, sell them yourself, or give them away in exchange for a charitable donation.

Invite the local media, ask a friend with a high-quality camera to be the evening's official photographer, and take lots of pictures (which you can later share on your website or social media sites).

6. Investing in paid advertising

Does advertising help sell books? Opinions are mixed about this, but myriad advertising opportunities exist, and some authors consider advertising a critical part of their marketing budget.

Your publisher may spend its advertising budget, if one exists, on advertising in trade publications for bookstores and libraries, or on "co-op marketing" at bookstore chains and collectives. (What, you thought that books made it onto those eye-catching tables or were pictured in those mass-mailed flyers for free?) These are big investments, and can make a critical difference in how well your book sells in bookstores.

Options like co-ops and catalogs aren't directly available to authors, but there are plenty of other channels for paid promotions that can get your name and book in front of consumers. Many authors invest heavily in search engine ads, banner ads on book- or audience-related websites and social media sites, print ads in magazines, and sponsored articles on websites, which don't look like ads.

Occasionally, an ad generates a noticeable sales increase. Usually, it doesn't—unless it's tied to a specific, special offer. Readers don't buy a book because they saw a picture of a book cover or description of a book in a sidebar. But if there's a limited-time giveaway, contest, or sale price, or of you want to promote a recent award or follow up on a major media hit, an ad can help you spread the word.[5]

It's easy to spend more money here than you can expect to recoup through book sales, especially on a new or untested book. This is why most book advertising on major outlets tends to feature books and authors who are already popular—they're reinforcing the brand among people who already know it, not launching it.

---

[5]Should you spend money on a Facebook ad or try one of those new e-book promotion websites? Is a print ad in the Kirkus catalog worth the money, or should you spend the money on Google AdWords? It's hard to answer this in a timely way, since the tide shifts often with advertising. What works today may be oversaturated and less effective next week, let alone by the time you read this. At http://bethjusino.com/resources I have an up-to-date page of recommended resources, which will track what services and opportunities my clients recommend, as well as the recommendations of other readers.

7. Giving books away #1

The most valuable marketing tool you have to promote your book is the book itself. As soon as you hold your new release in your hands, either in paper or on your e-reader, start thinking about how you can get it to influencers who might be willing to share your book with their audiences.

This might mean:

- Book bloggers. Remember those book bloggers we talked about in chapter 5? Influential bloggers can get your book in front of your earliest readers, and there are dozens of success stories from authors who "broke out" after a popular website recommended a book.

  Some authors or publishers will hire a company to do this for them as a blog tour, but it's a time-consuming project to carefully read each blog's submission guidelines and recent reviews to determine if it's a fit, and then to reach out with a personal note that introduces the book and offers a complimentary copy. The good companies who do it aren't cheap, and the cheap companies that offer "blog tours" usually aren't good. If you're considering hiring a company to solicit reviews on your behalf, take a good look at what they're offering. Will they solicit actual reviews from real readers, or are they promising a guaranteed number of "cover reveals" and generic book listings? Some unscrupulous web marketers reportedly take their clients "on tour" by posting information about a book on multiple sites that the publicity company owns themselves. It looks like your book is being marketed, but no one new is seeing it or buying it.

  If cost is an issue, you can also organize your own outreach to bloggers and book reviewers. Many, though not all, reviewers accept polite, professional queries from authors themselves, and a personal touch gives you the chance to build a connection that will last. If seeking reviewers this way appeals to you, set a realistic long-term goal of identifying and pitching a few reviewers per week for a set period of time.

- Influencers. Are there organizations, places of worship, nonprofits, or businesses that would appreciate your book? These might be small and local—the local senior center might appreciate your inspirational book for grandparents—or large and national—like sending the memoir about losing your father to Alzheimer's to the National Alzheimer's Association. Send autographed copies with personal notes to executive directors or local leaders, thanking them for their work and explaining why this book is a good fit for them. Politely ask that if they like the book, they will share it with their audience or provide an endorsement quote for you to share on your website and marketing materials.

Most of the books you send out for these purposes will disappear, but a few may find receptive audiences and Attract new readers. These are pebbles thrown into the pond—the ripples may go much farther than you ever imagined.

8. Giving books away #2

Influencers and bloggers have obvious megaphones to help you spread the word about a book, but don't forget about the readers themselves. When the problem to overcome is discoverability, often the solution is to get lots of books out there and into reader hands, and then let the word-of-mouth marketing take hold.

Seeding free books with enthusiastic readers, usually through large giveaways at conferences and other events, has been a strategy of publishers and authors for years. Late-blooming bestsellers like Donald Miller's memoir *Blue Like Jazz* found their audiences through giveaways several years after they debuted. But book giveaways have gotten a lot of extra attention since Amazon's Kindle Direct Publishing program and other sites made it easy (and free) to give away e-books.[6]

---

[6]If you're self publishing your e-book, you can join the Kindle Direct Publishing program (https://kdp.amazon.com/), where, at least for now, in exchange for agreeing to distribute the e-book version exclusively through Amazon, you have the opportunity to offer your book for free or at a discounted price for a few days each quarter. The most popular titles give away tens of thousands of copies, resulting in a surge of reader reviews and a sales bump for an author's other titles and for the book itself, once the giveaway ends.

Some authors dispute giving books away to readers on the principle that they're cannibalizing their own potential sales. Others will passionately argue that the extra reviews and exposure lead to more paying customers. Either way, e-book giveaways are starting to over-saturate the market, and their effectiveness may be waning.

If you choose to do a giveaway, be strategic. Wait at least three to six months after your book releases to Convert all your existing fans and audience into paid sales. Choose a time period when you'll be available to promote the program and help get the book in front of new audiences (this is when a paid ad might help you). Let your own fans and mailing lists know about the program, and ask them to tell their friends.

Amazon's not the only channel for book giveaways, either. Publishers have their own opportunities to negotiate sale prices and discounts with retailers for promotion purposes, and authors have plenty of other ways to seed books into reader hands. Sites like Goodreads and NoiseTrade have giveaway programs. Check my website for up-to-date reviews and recommendations for current programs.

9. Using video to promote the book

Book trailers are videos that preview and promote books, similar to the way that movie trailers entice watchers to see the latest blockbuster. There's one obvious catch, though: because books don't naturally have strong cinematic visuals that can be used in a trailer, book trailers often suck.

But they don't have to. Video can be an effective magnet if it's used right. A short trailer or promotion piece is easily shared online, grabs the attention of a YouTube-loving audience, and creates a dynamic way to deepen your book's experience and appeal. A video also gives you an interesting element to add to appearances and speaking events, as well as your website and other online social author pages.

But for a trailer to work, it needs to offer something unique. Effective book trailer videos must be more than your cover copy text superim-

Again, the details change often, so check the website to find out more.

posed over awkwardly-placed stock photos and bad, royalty-free music. If you've ever seen book trailers, you know the ones I'm talking about. Those videos are the same as a bad cover design when it comes to Attraction: they turn off readers before they even get to the first page.

Instead, a promotional book video should stand alone as an interesting piece, while also supporting the book. Think about recording an author interview (either audio or video) that provides a deeper look into your reason for writing this book: what's the back story, or what surprised you? You could also interview readers about how the book changed their lives, or offer "behind-the-scenes" tours of your novel's settings or characters.

This kind of project takes more time and effort, and it requires someone who's comfortable with a video camera and editing software, but in the end it gives you a product that is interesting for the audience—and that's always the main goal.

What appeals to you? What can you incorporate into your marketing plan? If a person needs to be exposed to a brand (your name and your book) multiple times before he or she makes a purchase, what can you do to build those positive impressions, and move closer to that book sale?

Your turn

- Is there an event or holiday tied to your book? Identify two or three key dates that you could use as centerpieces for your book promotion efforts in the next year. Think about how you could coordinate your Attraction efforts to gain more momentum.

- Make a list of at least ten influencers who might support your book. These might be groups or individuals with their own audiences, who have a strong connection to you and your book topic. How can you get your book to them?

- Start to prioritize your ideas and see how they fit together. What could you do to Attract readers this week/the week of the book launch? What can you do next month that will complement that activity?

8

---

hey, lady, wanna buy a book? converting sales

"We forget that the simple gesture of putting a book in someone's hands can change a life." — *Kate DiCamillo*

"You don't close a sale, you open a relationship if you want to build a long-term, successful enterprise." — *Patricia Fripp*

Y ou've been on TV, you've given away books, you had a great time at your launch party. You're doing a steady stream of promotional events that raise your visibility. So where are the book sales?

Being a familiar brand doesn't do you much good unless you can give your curious audience something to do with their knowledge. Your marketing plan needs to not just get your name out there; it has to ensure that you have the tools in place to sell some books.

There are two critical aspects book sales, which you may or may not control, but which we need to talk about.

- **The price.** If you're working with a publisher, they will set the price. If you are your own publisher, you can decide, within reason, how much a reader should pay for your book.[1] What will be low enough to attract sales, but still high enough to cover costs? What conveys the work's quality while still encouraging curious shoppers to take a chance on a new author? There are no easy answers here, and there are plenty of different opinions. One way to make an informed decision is to consider your competition among other new authors in your genre. Literary fiction readers, for instance, are usually willing to pay more for a book than readers in genres like romance or mystery. And established bestsellers can expect loyal fans to pay more. As you build your audience, you can raise your prices.

- **Where will you send people to buy your book**? This has become one of the most loaded questions in publishing, as authors and customers alike become deeply divided between Amazon and Everyone Else.

  Here's my advice: Amazon is big, but it's not universal. The best estimates are that Amazon sells between 30-50% of all books in the United States—less than half. Unless you've intentionally decided to an exclusive agreement with Amazon, provide links on your website, in your print material, and in interviews to various retailers that carry your book. That might mean Barnes & Noble, IndieBound (the online network of independent bookstores), Kobo,

---

[1] This is an important thing to consider when you're making self publishing choices. One sign of a scammy vanity press company (the kind that's there to fleece writers, rather than help them) is when the company that has already charged an author for basic publishing services like editing and cover design also insists on setting the book's retail price several dollars higher than other similar titles. Even with "author discounts," writers end up paying astronomical sums for their own books, and readers shy away from hefty price tags. Always, always research a publisher before you agree to work with it. The book you save may be your own.

iBooks, etc. If a local bookstore or specialty outlet supports you, mention them, too. (Especially if part of your personal marketing plan involves trying to network with local bookstores for events or book coverage. It's bad form to hand an independent bookseller an info sheet that's splashed with "Buy my book on Amazon!")

Once you have the logistics in place, here are other key tools to help readers commit to you and to your book.

1. Your website

You need a website. Period.

Even if you're choosing not to do any other online marketing, you need a website. (Actually, you need a website *especially* if you're choosing not to do any other online marketing.)

Your website is the always available outlet of up-to-date information about you and your book, and it's also the place where you make it easy for visitors to take the next step—to buy your book, to subscribe to your newsletter, to invite you to speak to their group, to share their experiences with others. You should have links to your website on every other place you talk about yourself: as part of your author bio in the back of your book, on your printed book promotion material and personal business cards, on your social media pages, on your press releases, in your advertising, and wherever else you share your work. However people find out about you, they should be able to navigate back to your website, and from there to their retail outlet of choice.

A website doesn't have to be flashy, expensive, or involve a lot of super-technical gadgets. But like your book cover, it should be well-designed and convey a professional image that appeals to your audience. Romance writers need different website colors, fonts, and styles than military thriller writers. And if you're writing both, you need a pen name for at least one genre and separate websites for each so you don't confuse your reader's expectations.

Present clear links on your home page and throughout the site to purchase your book (using the advice above about providing shoppers with options), but also give visitors enough unique content that adds value to their visit. Think about your website like the "special features" section on a DVD movie (remember those, back before everything was streamed online?). Not only do you need the basic information about your books and your bio, but you also need to give the visitor commentaries and behind-the-scenes information:

- Interviews: write a fun Q & A to help readers get to know you better.

- Deleted scenes: was there something that you cut from the book? Offer a deeper look at your characters.

- Extra information: Is your book set in a particular place? Add a page of details, maps, and interesting facts.

- Previews of future books: get your visitors excited about what's coming next… and then ask them to sign up for your mailing list.

- A calendar of upcoming events and author appearances.

- Links to reviews and articles.

- Resources for book clubs and discussion groups: questions, soundtrack music, snack ideas (seriously—the power of food is almost as important as the power of a good visual image).

A website doesn't need daily maintenance or attention, but it should be regularly updated so visitors know that you're actively writing and publishing.

2. Crowdfunding

Typically, crowdfunding happens before a book is released, as a way to build enthusiasm and raise the necessary funds to make the book a reality. (Some of you may be reading this book because you supported our campaign on Pubslush.com. If so, thank you again.) The most popular site for crowdfunding is Kickstarter, but other options like Indiegogo and Pubslush are also building reputations for working well specifically with authors and the book community.

The process of crowdfunding deserves a book in itself, and if you're interested, there are a number of good ones to check out. But the basic premise is that you take a specific need (i.e., covering the costs of self publishing, funding a research tour to develop the book's content, or funding a postproduction book giveaway to a charitable audience) and then create a web page asking your supporters to donate to the cause. You set a target of how much money you need and provide "rewards" for the backers—usually autographed copies of your published book or book-related gifts. Rewards can be as small as a thank-you email or as large as a personal appearance from the author. What type of rewards you offer will depend on your project, your needs, and your creativity.

Why is crowdfunding a "Converting" project? Because not only do you raise needed cash, but crowdfunding is also a fantastic way to build an early-adopting, committed community of supporters. These are the folks who will always feel like they knew you before anyone else did and like they were a part of your journey, rather than just another consumer. Your crowdfunding backers will be the strongest supporters you ever have.

But—and this is a big "but"—it's a lot of work. Managing and promoting your crowdfunding efforts requires a separate marketing plan and outreach effort, and it's an intense, time-consuming experience. So if you want to tackle this, set aside the time to do it right. (It's not a good idea, for example, to go on vacation for two weeks in the middle of your crowdfunding project. Trust me on this.)[2]

3. Online author pages

Provide as much information as you can, as close to the points of sale as you can

Most online retail sites have ways for publishers to add not only a general description of your book, but also editorial reviews, author videos, website links, and more. Amazon invites all authors to be part of Author Central, and Goodreads.com offers the Author Program, where you can

---

[2]What, you thought book marketers would do everything right to market their own books?

add a detailed author bio and links to your blog, social media, event calendar, and more.[3] Your local bookstore might also have programs for authors. Setting up these pages is a one-time investment of effort that might provide that extra nudge a reader needs to commit.

4. Bookstore outreach

Most sales for emerging and debut authors will happen online, where you don't have to compete for shelf space. But many readers I talk to don't feel like they've "made it" until they see their book on a physical bookstore shelf.

That's not a bad thing. More than half of all "paper" book sales happen in physical stores, so there's money to be made there. And when your book is stocked in a bookstore, your discoverability exponentially increases.

So how do you get a bookstore to carry your book?

Being listed in a distributor's catalog (through your publisher or through one of the larger companies like Ingram or Baker & Taylor) is a good start, but don't assume that just because a book is *available* to a bookstore that the bookstore will see any reason to order it. Remember, your book released on the same day as 1,500 other titles.

What can you do to increase your chances? Show them that you're an author with a plan.

Bookstore decision makers are understandably cautious about taking risks with their limited shelf space and may need to be convinced that your book is a potential moneymaker for them. Start with the bookstores that are closest to your home or that have some connection to your content. That is where your sales will be best, and local bookstores generally like to support local authors and books.

Call ahead to find out who you should speak to about stocking your title, and then visit in person if possible. The bookstore owner may or may not have time to talk to you, so be prepared to leave a sales packet of information: a single copy of your book and an information sheet

---

[3]Check my website, http://bethjusino.com, for links.

that lists the book information—especially the ISBN, the publisher, the distributor (where the book can be ordered), and the retail price. If you have received endorsements from published authors, media coverage, or positive reviews (especially from professional sources like *Publishers Weekly*, *Kirkus Reviews*, or *Library Journal*), add those to the info sheet.

That's what Mary did. She wrote a mystery series set in the Orcas Islands, a remote vacation getaway in the Puget Sound between Washington state and Canada. When her books debuted, she took them to every bookstore on the islands and to the mainland stores near the ferry terminals. She described the regional setting and shared the strong early reviews she had from readers. The bookstores, always interested in local and regional content, stocked the books and promoted them to tourists looking for a vacation read. Mary has seen steady sales ever since.

Most bookstores prefer to order books through the publisher or wholesale distributor.[4] Some smaller bookstores may agree to shelve your books on consignment—that is, you provide copies of the book, and when they sell, you and the bookstore split the profits. Consignment sales do have a financial risk; after all, you're paying all the upfront money. But if the store attracts the kind of reader you seek, it may be an Attraction investment you're willing to make.[5]

5. Scheduling book signings

What happens when you mix a launch party with bookstore outreach? A book signing!

Historically (that is, pre-Internet), this was the best way an author had to reach out to new readers and personally promote a book. However, unless you're already famous it's tough to draw a crowd of strangers. A tour of local bookstores across the country sounds romantic enough, but

---

[4]If you self published, make sure you know how your wholesale distribution is handled. Most independent presses and print-on-demand publishers are distributed through Ingram or Baker & Taylor, but some small presses use smaller, regional distributors.

[5]Consignment sales are different than the co-op payments discussed in the previous chapter. With consignment, you're not paying the bookstore to carry your book. You're providing them with inventory free of charge, and they're providing you with shelf space free of charge. When a sale is made, you both profit. Co-ops are a form of advertising, where you give the bookstore money that you won't get back, in exchange for shelf space.

even established authors have horror stories of readings where only one or two people showed up—and they were there for the food. Tours rarely recouped the financial investment a publisher put into them, so in this current frugal era, a publisher-funded book tour is almost nonexistent.

On the other hand, a well-managed bookstore appearance is a chance to build face-to-face relationships with both readers and booksellers. Treat every book signing event as a way to make a positive impression with the front line of retailers who hand sell and recommend books every day. Sign their in-house stock so they can advertise autographed copies. Talk to them, ask questions, and bring book-specific gifts or snacks.

Don't count on the bookstore to handle all the publicity for your event. Try to schedule book signings in areas where you have a personal base of friends and family who will help to promote it. Where do your most passionate influencers live? If your mother is already telling all of her friends about her famous author child, this is a chance to put her enthusiasm to good use. Ask her to help you fill the seats by inviting everyone she knows.

Another way to generate extra attendance is to join with other local authors and make it a group event. If four authors each promote a bookstore reading to their respective fan lists, then you have four times as many people in the room. Each author can give a short reading (no more than five minutes), and then collectively answer questions from the audience. Readers will be exposed to new authors, and the overall publishing community gets stronger.

If you love to travel and you can afford the commitment, you can extend local events to a full-fledged author book tour. One author I met at a conference had used Kickstarter to fund a cross-country road trip, stopping at every small-town, independent bookstore that would host him. He stayed connected to his fans and Kickstarter supporters through a travel blog of his trip and posted photos of his book (against various scenic and hilarious backgrounds) all over social media. It was an enormous commitment of time and resources, but that author made connections with retailers and readers who will remember him for years to come. And he developed some good content ideas for his next novel.

6. Reaching out beyond the bookstore

When you first sat down to understand your audience, you identified a number of places where they gather—and not just bookstores. Now that you have a book in hand, what can you do to meet them there?

Bookstores aren't the only places that sell books. What other retailers reach your audience? If your book is set in a picturesque vacation spot, would the gift shops like to carry a "local" story to sell to tourists? If you've written about sustainable gardening, does the local arboretum have a store? Would your memoir about parenting be appropriate for the maternity hospital gift store or a parenting magazine's "recommended resources" web store? Many new or independent authors find that their biggest retail supporters are those outside the bookseller world.

7. Personal appearances and back table sales

Book signings and personal appearances don't only happen in book stores. Pay attention to where you could host book-related events and directly sell your books. If your book features crafting, find out if the local craft store would be interested in holding a book signing and special crafting night, and sell your books while you're there.

If your novel would be a good fit with book clubs, research all the book clubs in a 100-mile radius of your home, contact them, and offer to attend the group for an exclusive author visit to answer their questions and autograph their copies if they choose your book. (Extend this offer nationally or internationally by offering to attend groups virtually, via Skype or other video conferencing.)

If larger critique or writing groups are in your area, offer to make a personal appearance at their meetings.

Converting readers and improving your sales is about much more than splashing "Buy My Book" messages all over the place. What other ideas do you have to make it easier for curious customers to commit to you?

Your turn

- What will you do to Convert new readers to your book?

- Visit ten of your comparative authors' websites (those who are writing for the same audience). Take a critical look at what they're doing. What do you like? What could you incorporate into your own website?

- Make a list of the bookstores (both chain and independent) in a fifty-mile radius of where you live. (If you're unsure, visit the major bookstore chain websites and the independent bookstore directory at http://www.indiebound.org.) Does your target audience shop in these stores? If so, what can you do to connect with them here?

9

---

the five star effect: transforming readers

"People share, read, and generally engage more with any type of content when it's surfaced through friends and people they know and trust." — Malorie Lucich, former Facebook spokesperson

W HAT makes a person decide to buy a book? Is it the cover art? Is it because they saw an ad or heard a radio interview, or because they thought the price was right? Sure, in part. But the most common motivator for a customer to purchase a book is this: *someone they trust recommended it.*

As we've seen, human beings need social proof. We want to know that whatever risk we're about to take with our time and money is safe and worthwhile because others have gone before us. While there's a certain sense of loyalty and enthusiasm that comes with being an *early* adopter, it's difficult for any creative project to draw that *first* adopter.

The first patient who agrees to an experimental, never-performed surgery.

The first pilot of a new airplane design.

Or that first person to invest in an e-reader, believing that the future of books would be screens instead of pages.

Along the same line, most readers will hesitate to be (or to feel like) the first person to buy your book. They need to believe that you already have readers, and that those readers had positive experiences, before they'll take the plunge.

How can you help them see that? By making sure that the positive experiences and good opinions of others are a key part of your marketing plan. That's transformation.

Here are some ways to capture—and Transform—those good experiences.

1. Using the pages at the end of the book

Your reader just finished your book. Her heart is still pounding from your action-packed climactic scene, or she's reveling in the new sense of hope she found in your insights. Before she closes the cover and gets distracted by the dirty dishes or the dog that needs to be walked, hold her attention for a few more pages.

At the end of your book, include:

- A specific request. Average book readers have no idea how important their opinion has become. Don't be afraid to ask them to go to Goodreads, Kobo, Amazon, or wherever they browse for books, and write an honest review. (Don't guide their message or ask them to leave a good review. You want honest feedback, no matter what. Respect their experience.) Remind your readers that if they're not online shoppers, they can also make their opinion heard by letting their local bookstore or library (wherever they found the book) know what they thought, or they can even email a review directly to you, the author. What a great way to show readers you value them.

- A specific offer. Draw readers further in by offering them something unique. For example, "If you go to my website, you will find 'deleted scenes' that didn't make the final edits." Or "Check out my Facebook page, where you can see a photo album of the families I interviewed for this book." Or "If you sign up for my newsletter, each month I'll send you a link to my podcast, where we explore the latest gadgets and how they stack up to the predictions I made here about the future of technology."

But don't ask them to do all three—too many offers will overwhelm your reader, and actually make it less likely they'll do anything. Prioritize your goals into one clear message, based on what you expect your target reader will find most valuable.

- Your author bio and photo, along with your website address. Readers want to know more about who you are.

- Acknowledgments. Remember to thank your early readers, influencers, and those who helped you bring the book together.

- A one-page teaser about your next book, if you're working on one. Keep the release date vague if necessary ("Coming Soon"), but start to build anticipation with a paragraph description, or the first page or chapter of the manuscript, or whatever you have. Send readers to your author website for more information and to sign up for your newsletter so they can be notified when it releases.

2. Sharing every positive reader story you can, in as many places as you can

Whether it's in your website, social media page, print materials, or newsletter, take advantage of every chance you're given to celebrate great stories. Excerpt your favorite reader reviews. Share (with permission) excerpts of emails you get or conversations you have with readers. After you visit a book club, share the best question that someone asked (and how you answered it).

"Celebrate" is key here. Approach this activity humbly, grateful for every reader you have and for the time that each person spent responding to the book. Let these joyful moments stand alone; don't use them to ask for anything. Make your fans feel like they're part of a community, and let them know that you value them and their feedback.

3. Knowing what people are saying about you

Transformation happens when someone blogs about their new favorite (or least favorite) books. As much as possible, track your media exposure to stay engaged in those conversations. Create Google Alerts (http://google.com/alerts) that email you whenever your name or book title is mentioned online, and regularly search social media sites (even the ones you don't regularly use) for your name or book title.

If you find yourself mentioned in a positive context (a good book review or a recap of an event or article), then thank the writer, either on the website itself if commenting or responding is possible, or through a personal email. Take five minutes to let the person know that you're grateful for his or her feedback.

But of course, not everyone is going to love your book. That's okay. If you see a bad review or a negative comment, the best thing to do is sit on your hands. Do nothing. Too many authors get caught up in online shouting matches because they didn't like what someone said, but getting defensive draws more attention to negative comments and makes you look petty and unprofessional. Unless you're faced with a professional, paid journalist who got a fact wrong, let it go.

I'll go even further, and suggest that you consider your first 1- or 2-star reader review as a badge of honor. Those occasional "dings" can even help your long-term success. Think about it: if you only have a handful of glowing ratings, then someone might suspect that only friends and family are writing reviews of your work. But when someone tears into the book—especially someone who shows his or her bias in the response—then it's clear that you've reached the mainstream.

4. Sharing photos

Here's a tip I rarely see highlighted in conversations about book marketing, but I've seen it work for authors over and over in real life: Don't underestimate the power of an image.

We're writers, so of course the written word reigns supreme, but remember that earlier quote from Smashword's Mark Coker when he talked about book covers? People are drawn to images. If you liberally use pictures and illustrations in your marketing efforts, you'll draw more eyes, and they'll stay longer.

What kind of photos should you use? Here are some ideas:

- Pictures of you with your readers. If you have a book launch party, assign a volunteer to take pictures of everyone having a great time. If you're invited to speak at a book club, get a shot of yourself standing with the group. Do the same with book signings, writers' conferences, and anything that shows you and your readers. Every time you have an event, make sure there are pictures of you with your fans to share on your website, your social media pages, and in your marketing materials.

  I know a novelist who, from her very first book signing, had a volunteer take her photo with every person who came to her table. In each shot, she'd either hold her book, or they'd stand in front of a six-foot banner image of her book cover. Then she'd give the people cards with her website address (this was back before social media; today it would work better on Facebook), so that after the event fans could download and share the photo of themselves with the (almost) famous author. It created a personal touch, bringing the author out from behind the barrier of the signing table, and to a place where she was face-to-face with her fans. And it gave readers a motivation to go to her website, where they'd also find information about her other books and bonus features. And finally, it gave her fans something to share with their friends. People like to share photos of themselves. Who knows how many thousands of new readers were Attracted to this one author when they saw transforming pictures of their friends looking happy and standing next to her?

- Casual pictures of yourself. I'm not recommending that you share bathroom mirror selfies or vacation pics in a Speedo. But push past the "official" author photo and get a little more personal. If your book is set in Washington, DC, share that shot of you standing in front of the Washington Monument when you were six years old. When the first case of a new release shows up at your front door, take a picture of you opening it and holding the first book copy. If you're deep into writing the next book and can't think of anything interesting to say to your fans, have someone take a funny snapshot of you at your desk, surrounded by books and piles of papers (or cats and empty wine bottles, or whatever your audience will appreciate as writing accessories).

- Pictures of your readers. Have some fun and spread the social proof. Ask your readers to share pictures of themselves with your book. Make it a contest, and award prizes to the most creative shots (In a pool? On a camel?) or the most appropriate setting (Inside a jail cell for a police thriller? At 30,000 feet for a travel memoir?). Collect and share these pictures on your website or social media, building a greater sense of community and connections among your readers.

  An alternative approach for children's book writers, since photos of young readers might not be appropriate because of privacy concerns, is an art contest. Ask your fans to submit their own illustrations or interpretations of your characters, and then share your "favorites"—all of them! Use only first names and last initials.

- Turn your text into images. Take a few favorite quotes from your book and turn them into images, with fancy fonts and interesting backgrounds. Dozens of websites will help you do this for free, and you can download the picture to share on social media or on a website. Your fans are more likely to share something that's visually appealing as well as intellectually interesting, and your words will reach more people.

5. Watching the bestseller lists

Famous lists from national outlets like *The New York Times* or *USA Today* are the gold standards of "bestseller." But online retailers (Amazon, Barnes & Noble, Kobo, etc.) have their own sales rankings that change daily and sometimes hourly. The higher you're ranked, the easier it is for readers to find you when they're browsing—and the more seriously they take you and your book.

If you hit a bestseller list—in print or online—make sure you have a copy of the print page or a screen shot, and then share it. Becoming a "bestseller" will increase your visibility and lead to even more sales.

6. Submitting your book to established awards

Another Transformative phrase to be able to claim is "award-winning," especially if you've won a prestigious or nationally recognized award. And there are plenty of awards out there, for every type of book.

Typically, you need to submit a title for awards, either in conjunction with your publisher or on your own, within a year of its release. If you're self publishing or looking for contests on your own, be careful; plenty of shady websites prey on authors who are anxious for recognition. Their "contests" come with high entry fees, but almost no visibility. Be selective, and look for awards that are recognized and recommended by other writers and writing communities. I prefer to invest in established awards like the IPPY (Independent Publisher) and the Independent Book Publishing Association's Benjamin Franklin Awards. Many genre-specific organizations and audiences also sponsor awards in their own categories, like the Bram Stoker Awards for horror, the RITA awards for romance, Books for a Better Life Awards for inspirational nonfiction, or the many awards given by the Society of Children's Book Writers and Illustrators.

Transforming positive reader experiences is usually the part of marketing that authors most enjoy, sometimes so much that they don't even remember that they're marketing. This is the place where you really can have some fun.

Your turn

- Get used to the idea of using photos to connect with your readers. For one day, carry a camera around with you. If your book is already published, take pictures of it in interesting places or with unusual people. Or create a "day in the life of an author" series of pictures, showing your work spaces and what it takes to put a book together. You don't have to share these pictures, but use them to think more about what you like to see in a person's photos and what you don't. What will make your readers smile?

- If your book is already published, look at your online reviews and choose two of your favorites to share. Add them to your website, thank the readers on social media, or find your own way to add them to your marketing messages.

- What will you do to Transform your book's readers?

part three

putting it all together

In which I synthesize the ideas, facts, data, and instructions I've given you, hopefully before your head explodes from all the information, and summarize what you should do with it.

part three

making it all
together

10

making YOUR plan

"There are no magic wands, no hidden tricks, and no secret handshakes that can bring you immediate success, but with time, energy, and determination you can get there." — *Darren Rowse*

"I TRIED marketing," a frustrated science fiction novelist told me not long ago. "I paid a publicist a lot of money, and she got me featured in a major newspaper article. But the sales dropped off right after that, and no one remembers it anymore."

"I tried marketing," said the anxious CEO-turned-business-writer. "We sent an email to all of our clients and customers. Thousands of names were on that list, and we sold a few copies. But the book isn't selling anymore."

"I tried marketing," explained the memoir writer. "I made one of those Facebook pages, but no one signed up for it, so I stopped posting. It didn't help me sell more books."

See what these situations have in common? The authors all depended on just a single action to carry the weight of their entire marketing efforts. Instead of a plan that balanced Attracting, Converting, and

Transforming, they threw everything into one thing. And then the one thing disappointed them.

So how can you avoid being these three writers? Well, by taking the last eight chapters and turning it into your own realistic, appropriate, and achievable marketing.

Let's make a plan

In case I haven't said this enough already: marketing is a marathon, not a sprint. Your book sales will come from the cumulative effects of multiple things that happen over time.

How many things? There's no answer to that. As we've already seen, there's no "magic bullet" that will slay the marketing beast and bring you royalties on a silver platter. Marketing happens gradually, piece by piece and reader by reader.

I get it. The very idea of long-term marketing can be overwhelming. If marketing is a steady tide, then there are always more things that you could be doing to market yourself and your books, always new ideas to try and new advice to follow. If you approach your book marketing efforts without a schedule and a plan, it's easy to burn out and stop doing anything.

That's why making a marketing plan is key to your book's survival. It's what keeps you sane and focused, and it's the way to keep track of what's important for you—and what's not. If something's not part of your plan, don't feel guilty for not doing it. And if it is part of your plan, then you'll know why you're spending your time there.

Plenty of books out there will tell you how to write a marketing plan that impresses other people. Ignore them. Your marketing plan doesn't have to be fancy. It doesn't need pie charts or tables or headings like "competitive analysis of high-potential accounts."[1] No one will grade you on this.

That doesn't mean that you can't add scrapbooking borders or spread-sheets, if that's what pushes your creative buttons. Or you can handwrite

---

[1] Yes, I actually found that phrase in a book about writing marketing plans.

it on a notepad that's smeared with jelly from the kids' lunches (or your own)—or on the next few pages here in the book itself. I'll give you space.

What matters is the content. For your marketing plan, whatever kind of book you're writing or wherever you are in the journey, you need to know six things:

1. Your audience (your market)

2. Your competitive place in that market (an analysis of where you're starting—how far does your platform reach? How does your book compare to others in its category?)

3. Your plan to reach your market (specific promotion strategies to increase sales)

4. Your budget

5. Your timeline (a realistic schedule of when you will do the things in #3)

6. Your expected outcomes

The first three things on the list should look familiar to you. We've worked through those already. But what about the rest?

What's it going to cost?

Ah, the dreaded question—and one that I can't answer for you. Your marketing efforts are going to cost you something, in some combination of time and money, but the totals of what you can invest are up to you. No amount guarantees success. I've seen authors spend a few hundred dollars and sell thousands of books, and I've seen authors disappointed after they invested thousands of dollars and sold only a few books.

But it's important to think about what you can spend. Small projects add up. Big projects can sound appealing, until you see the price tag. Is that high-dollar publicist really likely to draw enough media attention to make that retainer fee worth it? Watch the return on investment. From most perspectives, the author who spent $500 to sell 2,000 books is making out better than the author who spent $10,000 to sell 10,000 books.

As much as you can, you should track the results of each individual marketing effort to see how it affects sales. Before you spend thousands of dollars on a publicist, a paid ad, or a flashy website, ask whether the potential results will pay for themselves in long-term book sales revenue. If you're spending a dozen hours a week updating your social media, take a hard look at what you're getting from it. Are you drawing new readers?

A popular saying goes, "Quick. Cheap. Good. You can only pick two." If you're short on time, you can spend more to hire others to handle marketing tasks for you. (That might mean a professional, like a publicist for a media campaign, or an intern or assistant to handle the grunt work of managing mailing lists and scheduling.) If there's no money in the budget for others, you'll need to plan a lot more of your own time in order to promote the book well.

When will I do it?

Stephen Covey said it best in *The 7 Habits of Highly Effective People*: "The key is not to prioritize what's on your schedule, but to schedule your priorities."

I'm not recommending that you make a long list of deadlines to keep—or to miss and then feel guilty. Instead, a marketing schedule is designed to keep your projects under control, and prevent your marketing time and effort from becoming a tsunami that overwhelms you. A calendar keeps things realistic, because it reminds you that there are only seven days in a week, and twenty-four hours in a day.

Well, that, and you're more likely to stay on task if your marketing projects are scheduled activities and not just vague ideas.

Once you have the basic ideas from #3, of what you want to do to promote your book, take that list and hold it up to your calendar. How much time can you realistically spend on marketing in an average week? How many projects can you do in that time?

Again, there's no "right" answer here. But if you know your "author time" is limited to an hour every morning before the kids wake up and you head off to your day job, then a calendar will remind you that you won't be able to write a blog post, update all of your social media pages, and draft letters to three book bloggers in the same day. That's more like a week's worth of work, and that's okay. Take the marathon approach and look at your calendar for a whole year. This book of yours will be around for a long time.

What's most important to you and your readers, and what is time sensitive? If there's a deadline for a contest, a book festival you want to attend, a critical date for a press release, or other time-sensitive items, put those on the calendar first. Take the other, more flexible projects and fit them in where you can. If you're committing to a long-term effort, like blogging, decide in advance how often you'll blog, and then set aside the day or days you need for writing.

Many of my right-brained clients flinch when I talk about dates and deadlines. Calendars are not their natural friends. If it helps, remember that your schedule can be flexible, and if things take longer than expected or need to be rearranged, do that. Your marketing plan is your own.

Wait. I haven't even started yet, and you want me to know the outcome?

This last part is tricky. You've never sent a letter to book clubs asking if they want to read your book. How should you know how many of them will respond?

I get it. But I still want you to at least set some goals for your marketing plan actions, because if you don't know what you want to get from something, then you don't know why you're doing it. Identifying your desired outcomes is a safeguard against getting caught up in a marketing project because "everyone else is doing it" or "it's free, so it must be worth it."

What do you want to get from your Facebook page? What do you hope will happen when you send out that press release?

If you can't see how it will help you, skip it.

Outcomes should be quantifiable, but they don't have to be huge. For instance, if you are thinking about Twitter, your goal might be to attract

500 followers in the first year and to share content that at least three other people per week respond to or share with their own followers. If one of the goals of your website is to build a mailing list, you may try to attract enough traffic to convert 200 subscriptions in six months.

What if you don't meet your goal? Don't panic or despair. One of two things happened: either the effort didn't work (in which case you should re-evaluate whether to invest your time and money in that again), or your goals were off and need to be adjusted. Maybe you only garnered 100 newsletter subscriptions, but you can see that those subscribers are opening your emails and sharing your books. That's still a win, and now you know more about your audience.

It takes time to dial in your projects and expectations, and it's okay to adjust and change the marketing plan as you go along. It's a fluid document that should support your efforts, not limit them.

On the next page you'll find a worksheet that will help you work out your own marketing plan. Good luck!

Your Marketing Plan

Book Title:

Publication Date:

Genre/Category:
(This could be the BISAC code or the bookstore section where you'd find your book, or the section where your book will be listed on Amazon or elsewhere.)

Audience:
(If you're unsure how to describe your audience, go back to the questions at the end of chapter 2. What are their demographics? What books are they reading now? What do they do when they're not reading? Where do they gather?)

Product Strengths:

(What are your book's unique strengths? Why will readers like it and choose to recommend it over bestsellers in the same category? Knowing what makes your work special will help you develop your messages and promises. If you can't articulate this, neither can your reader.)

Marketing Budget:

(Be honest. There's no "right" answer to how much you should spend on marketing, and your plan has to fit within your budget. If you have $500, your priorities will be different than if you have $5,000. If you know you can set aside $100 a month, then you know that you need to spread out marketing efforts that cost money.)

Package Details

Design:

(If your book cover hasn't been designed, use this space to define what's important to convey on the cover. If the cover is done, mark this as "done." Make sure you have an electronic version of your final book cover design to use in marketing materials.

Cover Copy:

(Include the final, edited, proofread cover copy. If you don't have cover copy, use this space to brainstorm the important elements of character and conflict, or felt need and promise, to convey. The sooner you know this, the better you'll be at talking about your book, even before release.)

Endorsements and Blurbs:

(Do you have endorsements or blurbs on the book itself? If so, list them here, so that you can easily access them to include in your marketing materials. If not, brainstorm here a list of influencers who you could approach to write endorsements, and a date/deadline for when you will contact those individuals.)

Bonus Material

Check all the material that will be in your book, and then make sure it's completed

- ☐ Requests for reviews
- ☐ Bonus offer
- ☐ Author bio
- ☐ Acknowledgments
- ☐ Preview of your next book/Ad pages for previous pages

Price:

(What are the retail prices in all available formats?)

Formats and Outlets:

(Is the book available in paper and e-book formats in all outlets, or is it limited?)

Author Platform

(List the specific channels you're using—or will use—to launch your platform. If necessary, add more than the two spaces provided. If you're not sure, refer back to chapter 5.)

Channel 1:

Launch date:

Expected outcome(s):

Growth goals for the first year:

Growth plan:

How much time will you spend on this each week?

Channel 2:

Launch date:

Expected outcome(s):

Growth goals for the first year:

Growth plan:

How much time will you spend on this each week?

Promotion Plan (A-C-T):

(List the specific projects you will use—or are using—in each category to promote your book. If necessary, add more than the two spaces provided for each category.)

Attract Project 1:

Launch date:

What needs to happen before the launch?

Expected outcome(s):

Steps to complete (with target dates):

Attract Project 2:

Launch date:

What needs to happen before the launch?

Expected outcome(s):

Steps to complete (with target dates):

Convert Project 1:

Launch date:

What needs to happen before the launch?

Expected outcome(s):

Steps to complete (with target dates):

Convert Project 2:

Launch date:

What needs to happen before the launch?

Expected outcome(s):

Steps to complete (with target dates):

Transform Project 1:

Launch date:

What needs to happen before the launch?

Expected outcome(s):

Steps to complete (with target dates):

Transform Project 2:

Launch date:

What needs to happen before the launch?

Expected outcome(s):

Steps to complete (with target dates):

11

---

final questions and answers

Y ou've done it. You've evaluated your audience and product, developed a promotion plan, and created a plan and timeline for accomplishing it all. You're ready to market.

Still have questions? I thought so. Here are a few of the things that authors ask me most often, and my final observations and words of advice that didn't fit anywhere else, or that need more exploration.

Why isn't all of this marketing stuff my publisher's job?

I hear this lament from a lot of writers, both new and established. But as we've seen, the success of a new title, even one that comes from a Great Big Publishing House, rests heavily on authors' shoulders. It's *your* connections to readers that will help the book launch, *your* availability that will build a fan base and promote word-of-mouth growth.

Self-publishing evangelists say, "So if that's true, then there's no point to having a publisher."

Not true. Traditional publishers are authors' business partners in getting books to readers. And their primary jobs in the partnership are to (a) produce your book, and (b) get it onto bookstore and library shelves so that readers can find it.

Publishers bring value to authors through their financial investment in professional editing and packaging, industry knowledge, quality assurance, sales connections to retailers, and distribution opportunities. Those are difficult, and often expensive, endeavors. (Just ask any author who's published on their own.)

Most publishers do market books, as well. The publisher creates the book cover and writes the copy, which we've seen are two of a book's most important marketing tools. And a publisher's marketing team typically attends professional conferences and meetings that the average reader doesn't see. Publishers produce catalogs for bookstores and libraries. They try to get professional reviews. They promote their entire season's worth of books together.

Yes, larger publishers may invest serious money in a media campaign or a book tour to help raise the profile of an author they want to "break out," and they'll cater to the big-name authors with expensive ads and contests. But that's a perk they offer; it's not their primary role in their partnership.

We can all wish that publishers did more. Whether you have a contract with a mega-sized New York publisher or a small press with only a handful of employees, marketing budgets and staff are limited commodities, spread out over numerous books and authors all the time. At some point, you'll probably be disappointed.

But the sooner we realize that it's not the publisher's job to bring our readers to us, the sooner we'll be ready to go out and find them ourselves. Publishers are not failing if they don't build reader awareness. And if you can approach your relationship understanding that, you'll save yourself a world of frustration and disappointment.

Now that we got that out of the way, let's address a few other common things I hear from authors.

I have privacy concerns.

How should you balance your need to build a public reputation with your desire to protect your personal life? It's easier than you might think. Becoming a published author automatically puts you into the public sphere, but public speaking and online writing don't have to be more personally revealing than you want them to be. No one should ask for your children's birthdays or your Social Security number, and it's up to you what you want to share on your own website and in interviews. Work out in advance what you "author story" will be, and what you want your readers to know about you. Share as much as you're comfortable with. Readers want to know about an author, as well as a book.

If you're seeking publication, you need to acknowledge that certain pieces of yourself, like your photo and your bio, will be public. If you're building your platform in an informal place like social media, then you may find that you need to develop a more personal voice and to occasionally let your readers see pieces of your everyday life. That boundary is something you will need to establish for yourself.

I'm uncomfortable using computers.

I forget who said this first, but the principle holds: *If you're smart enough to write a book, you're smart enough to figure out Facebook.*

Like it or not, the computer is a critical tool of every twenty-first century writer's trade. And not just as a word-processing program. You need email to communicate with your publishing team, and it's important to understand how Amazon and the other major retailers interact with customers and authors. (If you've never searched for and bought a book online, stop reading right now and go do it. This is how many—and possibly most—of your readers will buy your book, and it's important to understand how the process works.) And then there's social media, a constantly changing piece of the online puzzle that's better to learn sooner rather than later.

If this baffles you, there are resources available to help. Community colleges and local libraries often offer enrichment classes to help people learn technology.

I don't have time to do anything except write this book.

This is a harder issue to address. As we've seen, the most important thing you can do to build your marketing success is to continue writing and publishing.

If your goal is to write a book, then that's where you should be spending your time, not in the sometimes distracting web of relationships and community connections. But if your goal is to become a successfully published author, then writing is only part of your job description. You also have to find your readers and share what you've written.

And last, but certainly not least, are these three tricks to being a Published Author:

- **You have to believe in your book before anyone else will.** I know a lot of authors who struggle with marketing, because they add caveats and qualifications when they think about their own works. *"I've learned a lot as an author, but I'm not as good as Author X,"* or *"I'm worried that readers won't like my book as much as Title Y."* Those thoughts trickle out in their marketing efforts, and readers can instinctively feel the hesitation.

  Publishing a book is not the time for false (or even real) modesty. Push past any inner criticisms or doubts, and toward a genuine belief that your book is one that readers will enjoy. If you're not ready to toot your own horn, start by collecting and sharing your positive reviews and responses from others. Don't hold back because "oh, readers won't be interested in seeing another 5-star review" or "that event isn't big enough for me to promote it." You've worked hard to get to this place in the publishing journey. Don't be afraid to share it.

- **Your sales and reach will probably grow gradually over time.** In the old publishing models, there was huge pressure for a book to sell a lot of copies in the first six weeks, or else bookstores would stop carrying it, and the book would go out of print. Now that the online bookstore shelves are limitless, books don't go out of print as easily, and there's room for slow, steady growth. Debut authors often have to wait weeks, months, and sometimes years to see a "sales spike" kick in, or when the right review, publicity hit, recommendation, or retail offer (or combination of all the above) suddenly pushes the book in front of a larger number of people. Be patient.

- **Your audience matters most**. More important than anything else that you read in this book is this: marketing is about understanding your audience, putting yourself in their shoes and understanding what they want. *This is more about them than it is about you.* If you understand your audience, then your marketing will find its target, and you will attract more readers and sell more books.

And there you have it. You now have the tools and tips to go and build a successful marketing campaign—and you might even enjoy it.

Want More?

Where do I find a critique group or writers conference in my area?

What websites do you recommend for advertising?

What publicity services are cost effective?

What online groups are worth joining?

What book awards are "legit?"

How do I find out more about podcasting/speaking/booking a blog tour?

In order to make *The Author's Guide to Marketing* as timeless as possible (which, given the speed publishing changes, means it will still be relevant a month from now), I've largely avoided recommending specific websites, companies, programs, or services. Today's popular new service will be oversaturated and neglected by next week. (Remember MySpace?) However, I have plenty of opinions about what's working well (and what's past its prime, marketing wise). And if you've been at this for any length of time, you probably do, as well.

Go to http://bethjusino.com/resources for my reviews and recommendations, or to share your own recommendations in marketing.

And while you're there, consider signing up for my mailing list to get regular updates about author marketing tools and resources, as well as information about my upcoming workshops (online and in person).

Guess what I'm going to ask you to do next?

If you read chapter 9, then you know what happens here.

Readers depend on the experiences and advice of others to know what resources are worth their time and money. Whether this book helped you or not, your opinion matters.

Will you please take five minutes and share a review of *The Author's Guide to Marketing* somewhere?

If you bought the book online, the easiest option is the retail site where you bought the book: Amazon, Barnes & Noble, Kobo, Apple, etc.

If you bought the book in an independent bookstore or at an event, there are plenty of other places where authors and aspiring authors are looking for information about good books:

- A community reading site like Goodreads or LibraryThing

- Your own blog or website

- Your library's website

Thank you!

About Beth Jusino

Beth Jusino is an editor, marketer, teacher, and writer who
loves words and the people who
write them.

A former literary agent and
magazine editor, Beth is now an
independent editor and marketing consultant, helping authors,
artists, and other innovators tell
their own best stories. She's the Director of Book and Author Marketing
for The Editorial Department, where she guides both traditionally- and
self-publishing authors through the maze of opportunities and pitfalls,
and she's a member of the Northwest Independent Editors Guild and the
Freelancers Union.

In addition to *The Author's Guide to Marketing*, Beth is the author
of several short e-books on publishing and marketing. She teaches a
quarterly "Guide to Getting Published" class at the University of Washington's Experimental College, and has spoken at dozens of conferences
and literary festivals across the country. She's been a contributing author
or ghostwriter to a variety of books, from story compilations to business
titles, and has been widely published in national magazines.

Beth grew up on the New Jersey shore and now makes her home in
Seattle with her husband Eric and their cat, Comma. (What else would
an editor name a cat?)

Visit her online at http://bethjusino.com
Twitter: @bethjusino
LinkedIn: http://linkedin.com/in/bethjusino/
Google+: http://google.com/+BethJusino

Acknowledgements

"Writing is a solitary experience, but it takes more than one person to make a great book." Creating (and publishing) *The Author's Guide to Marketing* made this sentence explicitly clear to me. This project never would have come about without the help and encouragement of these many people, to whom I am grateful.

To the women of MOPS International, my earliest mentors in writing, editing, managing, and marketing; especially Elisa Morgan, Carol Kuykendal, Karen Parks, and Michele Hall.

To the agents and staff at Alive Communications, who taught me the business of books: Rick Christian, Lee Hough, Don Pape, Joel Kneedler, and Cindy Wilson.

To my colleagues at The Editorial Department, who invited me to build an author marketing program from scratch, and then supported every crazy idea since: Ross Browne, Jane Ryder, Morgana Gallaway, Liz Felix, and Heather Goodwin.

To my beta readers: Jennie Spohr, Rajdeep Paulus, Jim Thomsen, Chip MacGregor, Sarah Jackson, Kristi Jenkins, Dana Twight, and March Twisdale. You gave me my earliest encouragement that there was really something valuable here, and your unique perspectives made it better.

To my PubSlush supporters, who invested generously in this book before it was even published: Roger Lucas, Jennifer Schuchmann, Beth K. Vogt, Max Slowik, Auburn McCanta, Molly Asher, Aya Walksfar, Cynthia Hartwig, Jeffrey Russell, Sana Quijada, Rajdeep Paulus, and Brooke Wright.

To the folks who made this a book: copyeditor Amanda Bauch, cover designer Kelly Leslie, and interior designer (and tech support, and emotional support 'til death do us part) Eric Jusino. Everything here that looks good is because of you. The mistakes are all mine.

And to the authors and aspiring authors, every single one of you, who have invited me to be part of your publishing journeys. I'm inspired by your passions to create, and I've learned the art of marketing with all of you. Keep pursuing your dreams.

CPSIA information can be obtained at www.ICGtesting.com
Printed in the USA
BVOW08s1306030714

358071BV00001B/2/P